LAND GIRL

Cover and overleaf: The author ready for action

L A N D
G I R L

Her story of six years in the
Women's Land Army, 1940-46

Anne Hall

Ex Libris Press

First published 1993
Reprinted 1994, 1996 and 1998 by
Ex Libris Press
1 The Shambles
Bradford on Avon
Wiltshire

Typeset in 10 point Palatino

Design and typesetting by Ex Libris Press

Cover printed by Shires Press, Trowbridge
Printed and bound in Great Britain by
Cromwell Press Ltd., Trowbridge, Wiltshire

ISBN 0 948578 34 3

To my sisters, Cara and Jill.

CONTENTS

1 Enrolment

15th June 1940

IT WAS MY SISTER CARA who persuaded me that we ought to volunteer for the Women's Land Army as she knew I had often thought I would like to work on a farm. We were both working in hospitals at the time, in Almoner Departments; Cara in a London hospital, and myself as a clerk in a Bournemouth hospital. Though we enjoyed the work we felt we could contribute more to the war effort on the land.

On Saturday 15th June, 1940 we took the plunge, and I became recruit number 33530. Though twenty-years-old I still lived at home as my weekly wage was £1 (18s.9d after deductions). The Hospital Secretary raised no objection to my leaving a 'Reserved Occupation', but the Almoner was concerned. He remembered well the dreadful experience of unemployment for ex-servicemen after the last war, and felt I was too impetuous in leaving a steady job, with fair prospects of advancement. My father shared the concern that we had acted impetuously, and though he had told us many delightful reminiscences about his boyhood joys on his father's Lancashire farm, he was now at pains to warn us that life as a farm labourer was very different from being a farmer's son. Our work would be heavy, dirty and arduous in all weathers, and he very much doubted whether we had the necessary stamina for farm life. I had been considered a delicate child, having had a mastoid operation after measles, and twice had bronchial pneumonia. This, however, did not prevent our doctor readily giving me the necessary medical certificate.

Twelve long days after sending the medical certificates to Miss Trotter, CBE, we received uniform measurement forms, and instructions to report for training to a farm in Herefordshire, on 15th July. The Hospital Secretary felt he was not given sufficient notice for me to leave straight away, but to my relief was persuaded to let me go in time to take up the training arranged. I received so heartwarming a send off that I found it quite hard to say goodbye to my work and colleagues.

Leaving home was going to be even more of a wrench. I had been surrounded by quite a large family in Bournemouth and I now faced the prospect of this upheaval in our family life with a mixture of sadness, anxiety and excitement. Our grandmother and two aunts lived near us in Southbourne. Aunt Mabel had recently moved to Bournemouth after the early retirement of her husband, and he had since died. Aunt Gwen and her family had lived with her mother since the death of her husband, so cousins Alan and Joan had always been our close friends. Alan had been in the Territorial Army and had now been called up to serve in the Royal Artillery. Joan was planning to leave home soon, having just become engaged to marry a work colleague.

Our brother Bill, a law student, was expecting his call up, having just sat his law final. Mother and Dad would still have our young sister Jill at home, as she was only twelve-years-old and still at school. The scattering of the family was sad for parents who had been through a similar experience in the last war, but the challenge of war was uppermost.

2 Training

July - August 1940

I HAD ALWAYS SUFFERED GREATLY with homesickness at boarding school, but having Cara with me and with a great sense of adventure, on 15th July we happily waved goodbye as we steamed out of Bournemouth to take up our period of training. Mother was left looking rather desolate, having seen off many to the war effort during the First World War.

On changing trains at Evercreech we were delighted to meet our brother Bill, on his way back to Bournemouth after a weekend visit to his fiancee Enid. Bill had just passed his Law Finals and was soon to be called up, so he was arranging for their marriage as soon as possible. We changed trains again at Hereford and then rode through lovely scenery to the small country station of Berrington and Eye. The station master greeted us and told us that Mrs Morgan, wife of our trainer farmer, was on her way to meet us.

Mrs Morgan drove us to our billet with Mr and Mrs Hackett, at Manor House Cottage. We were at once made to feel at home, with a very warm welcome from the Hackett family. Little Mary and John Hackett, aged five and two, treated us to shy smiles. We were shown to a comfortable and attractive bedroom, and were excited to find large parcels of uniform awaiting us, but as tea was ready the parcels had to wait. After tea Mrs Hackett walked us to the farm so that we would know where to go in the morning. We met Mr Morgan and he said he would expect us at 7 am the following day.

We were ready for an early night after all the day's excitement, but were a bit slow about getting to bed as we just had to try on the uniform. There were stiff hide, ankle lace-up boots, and gum boots with heavy cleated soles, khaki- coloured knee socks, brown knee

The Manor Cottage:
Mr & Mrs Hackett,
Mary and John.

breeches, fawn aertex shirts, green V-necked pullovers, khaki long-sleeved overalls and khaki dungarees. We liked the brown knee-length overcoat but did not feel so enthusiastic about the fawn hat with round brim, but approved the WLA tie and badge, and were glad to find a pair each of brown hide walking shoes. They would need a bit of working in as they had very thick stiff soles. We decided the dungarees and gumboots would be sensible wear for the cowsheds.

At 6 the next morning Mrs Hackett brought us a cup of tea. She found us awake and writing cards to post home on our way to the farm. We arrived punctually at Moreton Farm cowsheds, to find Mr Morgan, his sixteen-year-old son Geoffrey and Aaron, a farmhand, already hand-milking. We were told we could just watch. We remarked on all the cows' names painted over the stalls – Snowy, Fanny, Daisy, Primrose, Roan, and so on. Mr Morgan surprised us by telling us that the cows knew their own stalls, and would always go to the right one when entering the shed, though some were occasionally caught trying to steal food from the manger of another's stall before going into their own. The hand milking, seen done by experts, appeared easy enough, and we looked forward to having a go since the cows seemed very quiet and well behaved. We helped to unchain the cows, first having been warned to steer clear of their horns as they turned to leave the shed. We had the company of Geoffrey and the cows part of our way back to the billet, so knew which field was theirs when told to take them back.

After a substantial breakfast, Geoffrey taught us how to set about cleaning the cowshed, stressing the importance of hygienic conditions for milking. Geoffrey was expert at twisting the brush about to clean all the corners. Having brushed the stall debris into the channel behind the stalls, all the straw and dung was loaded from the channel into the wheelbarrow (wheeling the barrow was quite an art in itself) and taken to the dung heap which was kept for fertilising the fields at the right season. This done, the shed had to be hosed down and thoroughly swept until gleaming clean. We quickly realized we would have to work up a lot more muscle power before we could compete with Geoffrey's speed of working.

The cowsheds finished, we were invited into the farmhouse kitchen to enjoy a glass of milk and a bun, while having a chat with Mrs Morgan. Armed with pitchforks, Geoffrey then took us to a field of vetches which had to be turned over for drying. This looked a lot easier and lighter work, but by lunchtime not only were blisters making our hands sore but our backs were aching too. Mr Morgan must have suspected this when, to our delight, he gave us the afternoon off so that we could go to Leominster to get our ration books adjusted for Mrs Hackett's use. Mrs Morgan chided her husband for telling us to rub soil well into our hands to harden them.

"Oh. But they have such nice soft white hands," she said, "Girls don't want to spoil them, I'm sure."

We decided we were happy to do so, if it would spare us the blisters. We returned to the farm for the evening milking and were allowed to try our hand at milking the long-suffering Violet. Violet was a most good-natured and patient shorthorn though naturally reluctant to release much of her milk to two such awkward novices. We persevered, and when we eventually tackled Polly and Fanny and were able to obtain respectable pailfuls it was a great thrill, though we suffered aching hands for a week or two.

The daily chore of cowshed cleaning improved and we became expert with a yard broom, and at slinging buckets of water very effectively, so were able to get the job done quickly and to Mr

Morgan's satisfaction.

Mr and Mrs Morgan could not have been kinder to us, or more encouraging, and our days of training were wonderfully happy. I am sure we provided the farmhands with many a laugh too. Cara, suddenly asked to try to stop a cow about to leave the shed, flung her arms round Blossom's neck, only to be roughly thrown aside by the astonished and indignant animal.

One of my daily delights was to clean out the pig pens, though my new dungarees suffered from the friendly youngsters tugging at them as I worked. I always emerged from the pens with wet and meal-covered overalls, but I loved the playful pigs. Cleaning hen houses was an unpleasantly smelly business, but I noticed two hens were 'laying away' – one had a nest of nine eggs and another fifteen eggs in a hedge. Mrs Morgan tested the eggs for freshness by floating them in water, and discarding the ones that floated. She gave me a dozen that were good, to help Mrs Hackett feed two hungry Land Girls.

Each day, between milkings, there was field work of one sort or another. We learned the art of cutting back hedges with long-handled hooks and spent some hours at hoeing, clearing crops of thistles and docks and so on. We worked alongside Geoffrey and Aaron and Mrs Griffiths, a villager, and enjoyed their friendly banter and exchange of village news. On Sundays we were free after the early milking and shed cleaning so met the villagers by attending the village church. The Vicar was very welcoming and showed us round the church. We met the local WLA 'rep.' Miss Carver and she invited us to tea. Everyone seemed interested to hear how we enjoyed life 'on the land'. How we wished we could stay in this friendly village, and work at the Morgans' farm!

A letter from home brought the news that cousin Joan was to marry, before our training ended. As Joan had been like a sister from our early days we found it hard to accept that we must miss being with her on her great day. Since our training could not be interrupted, we had to accept this great disappointment. As a little consolation,

Aunty Gwen sent us a huge chunk of the wedding cake to share with the family in our digs. The children certainly enjoyed their share of the icing sugar, as we all did.

When we heard that our brother Bill and his fiancee Enid were to marry three days after our training ended, it cheered us to know we could be with them. Theirs was to be the usual 'Soldier's Wedding' in a Register Office as Bill had now received his call up, having successfully passed his law final. Sad though we were that it was not to be a dressy church wedding like Joan's, at least we would not miss it.

We were now experiencing our first harvesting of corn, but this was not quite the light-hearted picnic scene so often attractively portrayed in paintings. The hours of work were arduous and long, but a cheerful and enjoyable time nonetheless. Once a path had been cut round the field by farm men with scythes, in came the horses with the cutter and binder. We then set to work 'stooking' the sheaves thrown out by the machine.

We were shown how to push the sheaf heads firmly together with feet well apart, eight pairs of sheaves to each 'stook'. In this way the corn could dry out or at least better withstand the wind and rain. We quickly discovered our long-sleeved overalls a great blessing, since thistles in the stooks were painfully scratchy on bare arms. The stooks had to be turned inside out while drying to ensure the corn was dry enough for rick-making.

Farmhands from other farms and villagers with spare time, turned up to speed the work and add to the fun and the sense of added importance of the harvest, with the arrival of food from abroad uncertain with Merchant Navy lives lost through enemy submarine activity. When not harvesting there were still a few hay fields to clear, so the days went quickly. Cara and I were struggling to acquire the knack of lifting loose bundles of hay on the end of a two-pronged fork, and landing them safely and tidily, without allowing them to scatter all around. Cara made best progress at this art and spent her time in the field loading wagons, while I was at the farmyard helping

Mrs. Morgan.

to toss the hay off the wagon, to those building the ricks. I was impressed by their skill at packing each layer of hay evenly, with straight rick sides, and a tidy rick in the making.

Our last day on the farm was spent clearing a corn field. Towards the end of the day a WLA committee member came to tell us we were to return home until we heard that a suitable farm job had been found for us. She gave us free train travel warrants as our wage while training was ten shillings a week and free board. Farmers were not yet convinced that girls could prove useful to them and, as yet, not many of their men had been taken for active service.

We were sad to end our training and to leave the Morgans' farm on 10th August. We were rather discouraged to learn that, so far, very few requests had been received for Land Girls, though we looked forward to seeing our family and telling them about our life on the farm which had proved such fun. We found it hard to express just how grateful we felt for all the kindness at Moreton Farm, Eye, and in the village, and for the patient training and encouragement we had received from the Morgan family. It was a real wrench having to leave them. Geoffrey relieved the sad moment somewhat when he produced for each of us the tail trimmings of Roan and Snowy, beautifully bound with binder twine. We attached these cow tails to our breeches belts as a sort of graduation emblem, and were still wearing them when we attended the wedding ceremony of Bill and Enid in Weston-super-Mare a few days later. Though we corresponded with the Morgans for many years, we were sad that we never managed to accept their many invitations to us to visit.

3 Bishops Frome, Herefordshire

August - September 1940

TWO DAYS AFTER THE EXCITEMENT of a family gathering to celebrate the marriage of Bill and Enid, Bill was summoned to an Officer Training Unit in Belfast, then to a posting in Liverpool where he was to join a unit using Aintree Race Course. At the same time, Cara and I were glad to hear that we were to go, on 19th August, to work for Mr Dale at Bishops Frome, near Bromyard. We were glad to have another four days at home in order to see more friends, as we did not know when we might again get leave.

On the Monday we crammed ourselves excitedly into an already overcrowded train for Bristol. We had the company of a friendly airman next to us in the packed corridor, which relieved the tedium of slow travel. On the Hereford train we enjoyed the delights of the Herefordshire country, then at its most colourful with the autumn patchwork of reds and golds and greens across the fields.

We were met by Mrs Dale and her daughter at Hereford Station. Mrs Dale said we had time to browse round the city for a while, as they had some shopping still to do. We did a tour of the Cathedral and then we wandered round a few shops before returning to the Dales' Morris Eight for the ten miles or so drive to their farm. We were shown up to an attic room which was nice and light and large, with views over the farm. The sight of a double bed with flock mattress was a bit of a let down. Land Army regulations specified single beds for Land Girls. We did not like having to share a bed, but said nothing since we thought this was possibly normal accommodation for workers in the country.

We unpacked a little, then went down to tea. We met Mr Dale senior, and his son, Ellis, who now had charge of the farm, so was our boss. Ellis took us across to the cowshed as soon as tea was over and we were introduced to machine-milking. It seemed rather complicated, and we were glad to do the hand stripping after the machines were taken off. The most involved bit was the dismantling of the machines into so many parts, all ready for sterilising in the dairy. I was relieved when Ellis said he would be reassembling the machines until we got used to them. He assured us it was not diificult once we became familiar with them.

After milking we had a walk around to enjoy the glorious scenery. Despite the double bed and somewhat lumpy mattress we were soon sound asleep.

We were up at 6 am and sent by Mr Dale to fetch up the cows. When we eventually found the right field, some way from the farm, Ellis was already there and had the cows rounded up. The machines proved to be no great problem, and we appreciated the speed with which the milking was done. After breakfast, I drove the cows back to their field while Cara helped to clean the machines in the dairy. When Cara went off to the fields to tackle the familiar and boring job of pulling out docks and cutting down nettles and thistles, I was told I was needed in the farmhouse to help Mrs Dale. When I protested that I was an outdoor worker, I was sent into the yard to chop wood and bring in coal. When, after lunch, we were told to do the washing up, we refused, and explained that Land Girls were not allowed to take on domestic work. Though this was not well received, we were both sent to the field job until I fetched the cows for milking. Cara helped to chain them up.

When all were chained we washed the udders before going in to tea. When the evening milking was over we excused ourselves and went up to our room. We felt the Dales had really wanted to employ someone prepared to work indoors and out as there was a lot of work for Mrs Dale indoors, so we were already a disappointment to them, and as we were not prepared to take on the domestic work, we had better seek out our local rep. and see what she advised.

The pattern of work settled down with Cara helping to harvest corn and kept busy pitching for most of the day, though helping with the milkings also. I spent time between milkings harvesting plums in the orchard until it was time to fetch in the cows. I usually got them in and washed, ready for milking, just before tea each day. I was allowed to take the horses to the field after their day's work, and Mr Dale said he would let me do some riding when the busy harvest time was over. Ellis, noting I loved the horses, asked me the next day to take an elderly hunter, Mollie, to the blacksmith to be shod. He threw me up into the saddle, and I had a lovely ride.

At 4 pm I was delighted to be asked by Ellis to fetch Mollie from the forge and then round up the cows with her, as they were spread out over two large fields and were always a bit reluctant to leave their lush pasture. Mollie had a lovely temperament and had had a very good training – she was so well-mannered and responsive and so used to bringing up the cows that there was little for me to do but enjoy the ride and admire the way she kept the cows on the move, gently weaving from side to side behind them with no guidance from me. After that, I was often allowed to take Mollie to fetch the cows if she was not needed in the orchard to pull a light dray. When Mollie was not available the farm dogs, Laddie and Lassie, were a great help.

On Saturday we were given the afternoon off until the evening milking, so took the chance to go to see the local rep. and tell her how we felt the farm would not be suitable for us in the winter, as the pressure would surely then be on to persuade us to help indoors. Mrs Payne felt the farm did not meet the regulations set for employing Land Girls, and said she would see if a more suitable farm could be found.

We returned to the farm in good heart, encouraged by our rep's sympathy. We were delighted when Ellis then offered us a lift into Hereford for the evening: we decided we would go to a cinema. Ellis first took us into a pub for a drink, then left us after arranging to meet us outside . (He later told us he thought that would help us to 'pick up' a soldier, for a pleasant evening).

As it happened I suppose we did make a 'pick up' though it was

Peter Matthews of Bartonsham Farm, our Saturday friend.

not intended. We left the pub as we had been discouraged at home from entering pubs, but were rather dismayed to find all the cinemas already full. Fortunately, one of the cinemas had a cafe open until 11pm, so we decided on a rather drawn-out supper. We had not been there long when a nice young man joined us, wanting to know on which farm we worked. He owned Bartonsham Farm, Hereford, and his name was Peter Matthews. When he heard we had to wait until 11 for our farmer to give us a lift back, he not only kept us company that evening, but arranged to meet us there every Saturday – an event we soon looked forward to as our friendship flourished. Though they gained little profit from us, the cafe staff did not seem to mind, as they knew Peter well and paid him each Saturday for milk supplied by his farm.

Sundays were comparatively easy, as we were free, apart from milking times. After the morning milking on our first Sunday we amused ourselves watching Mr Dale working a terrier and a ferret together at rat catching. We lazed in our room in the afternoon, letter writing. When the evening milking was over we walked into Bishops Frome to see if there were buses to Hereford, but were unlucky, so we returned to the farm and early bed.

On Monday morning I was intrigued to see Ellis trying to break in a young horse that had not previously been ridden. After breaking the girths of the saddle, Ellis mounted at the second attempt and, despite the bucking, persuaded the horse to take off. When they returned, Ellis said he had had a good ride and that a paying guest, due in the afternoon, would be able to ride him, as he was an expert horseman. The arrival of the guests Mr Smith and Mr Lamb, who were middle-aged, cheered our spare time as they had a car and invited us to accompany them on drives round the country – we were treated to snacks and cider at the Hop Pole in Bromyard and taken to a film some evenings.

The kindliness of these guests helped us to settle better in the job. Our relationship with the family was a bit strained after our refusal to take on domestic duties, but the evening outings were a blessing to us, and maybe a relief to the family. We were at work once more on the corn harvest, and our work seemed to be accepted as satisfactory but, though we asked about our pay, it was not yet forthcoming and we were feeling the pinch, but did not like to press the matter.

News from home was about a lot of enemy activity overhead at night, but the bombers were heading for Southampton and London and those cities were having a dreadful time. Hereford also had been visited by bombers, and each night we watched the searchlights criss-crossing the sky. Ellis did night-time LDV (Local Defence Volunteer) duty from time to time, and rumours suggested the Germans were expected to attempt an invasion soon. (The LDV later had to change its name to Home Guard, and some said this was because of ridicule suggesting LDV stood for the 'Look, Duck, Vanish' Brigade. The new name seemed to be more pleasing to the members who were now getting into uniform, and becoming better equipped). Mr Dale was called out for Home Guard duty at 2 am on Sunday – a German invasion was expected and there was a nationwide flap.

By early September, the family had grown with the addition of Mrs Williams, Ellis's sister, and her little boy, Bobby. No doubt she had come to help her Mother with the housework as the guests would add to her duties. Bobby loved being in the cowsheds or helping to fetch up the cows – he was enjoyable company and a real help. During the week I had the added joy of being sent off on Mollie to find nine missing calves. I met Mr Smith out riding as I tracked down the calves, so he helped with rounding them up. I had plenty of opportunities for a canter, so really enjoyed myself. I had the additional morning job of cleaning the stables and the calf pens but we were never too tired for the evening out in Ledbury or Bromyard with the paying guests. On Sunday afternoon we said goodbye to our good friends Mr Smith and Mr Lamb as their holiday ended, and they were returning home to Tamworth. We missed them around the farm, and our evening jaunts.

Much of our time during the following two weeks was spent in

Cara relaxing after harvesting plums.

the orchards, harvesting apples or plums. We were pleased to be allowed to eat any over-ripe fruit, as the open air life gave us healthy appetites. On 14th September we heard from Mrs Hope-Hannyngton in reply to our letter telling her of our dissatisfaction with conditions at the farm, and she promised to come and see us the following week. However, our local rep. visited us and gave the Dales notice that we would be leaving in two weeks. That plan altered when the Dales asked us to leave on 21st September, as two former employees of theirs were returning to help on the farm and in the house, and they would need our room. On the Wednesday we were introduced to Leopold and Bianca, Austrian Jewish immigrant friends of the Dales, who were to take over from us on Saturday.

Our only regret at this short notice to quit was that we would not be able to keep our Saturday evening date with Peter Matthews. We would have liked to see him to thank him for his friendship during our stay in Bishops Frome. We did, however, keep up a correspondence with him for some years.

On those last few days we were kept very busy, and we worked hard, hoping to leave a good impression. We were set to work scrubbing down the walls of the cowshed, and then applying lime or whitewash with the help of a fire-fighting stirrup pump. We took turns in pumping or directing the spray over ceilings and walls and plenty, unintentionally, over ourselves. We sang joyfully as we worked, much to the amusement of old Mr Dale. He seemed very pleased with our efforts.

Our excitement and interest, watching a large old steam traction engine slowly lumbering into the farmyard and being manoeuvred into position by the ricks, soon changed as we were set to work helping with threshing for the next two days. It proved to be the least pleasant work we had yet been involved in. We soon had no love for that droning monster with an insatiable appetite for sheaves, belching out clouds of dirty dust, and rapidly filling heavy sacks of corn to be dragged away and replaced.

I was given an easy job – cutting bands off the sheaves to be fed into the monster. Cara had the worst of the threshing jobs: she had to clear chaff from underneath the machine. It proved to be the dirtiest task; she soon looked a picture of grime and resorted to wearing a scarf over nose and mouth. It made her look a real villain, and with her hair full of chaff I had a great laugh at her expense until I had my turn at the job.

Our last day was spent on the threshing of a bean stack, the dustiest job of the lot, and we were kept at it till 7 pm. After a quick tea the milking seemed restful in comparison, but we were very thankful to get indoors and finish our packing and room tidying, ready for departure early in the morning.

Our local Rep. had advised us to go home again to await word from County Headquarters as to where we were to go next. We decided to do this, though we were tempted to accept an invitation to visit the Morgans. We had so much luggage, and such dirty clothes after the threshing, home was the obvious place to make for. Waiting for a taxi to take us to the station quite early the next morning we said goodbye to Mr Dale, then paid our last visit to the cows, and there said goodbye to Ellis, Bianca and Leopold, all busy at the milking. Sad though I was to leave Laddie and Lassie, and the beautiful Mollie, who had given me much pleasure, our feelings were of relief rather than sadness – we clearly were not the workers the Dales had hoped for, and they must also have been relieved to have the efficient, experienced Austrian friends again working with them.

Maybe it was our tiredness but the journey home seemed endless. Having caught the 10.20 train to Gloucester, we had changes at Mangotsfield and Bath and then a slow train to Bournemouth. It was most cheering to find Dad waiting with the car.

Having been revived with a hot meal we kept the family amused with our tales of farm life, and had to admit to Dad that his warnings about life as farm workers had been no exaggeration.

4 Back to Base

September - October 1940

LIFE AT HOME IN THOSE two weeks was punctuated by several air raid warnings day and night. Our local shopping area in Southbourne Grove had suffered from raids, and on each of our visits to Bournemouth shops we found ourselves spending time in the various basements when the warnings warbled. We saw 'dog fights' over the sea, as our Spitfires chased after the German raiders, and watched shells exploding around the planes. Mother and I were startled when in the Grove to see a German plane flying down the centre of the street at less than roof height. Fortunately a Spitfire on its tail did not allow it to spray us with gunfire. Life certainly was full of excitement.

Despite the frequent raids we got about to see our friends. My colleagues at Boscombe Hospital were all so welcoming that I was a little sad I had left, especially as there did not seem to be much need of girls on the land yet.

We were more disheartened at receiving a letter of rebuke from Mrs Hope-Hannyngton for not waiting in Hereford to see her before returning home. In the same post arrived a letter from Bedford College (then evacuated to Cambridge) offering Cara a place on the Social Studies Course.

In view of the lack of work for Land Girls, it seemed to Cara the sensible thing was to leave the land and continue her training. I had to acknowledge the sense of this, but the thought of having to carry on in the Land Army on my own filled me with dismay, though I would not admit it. Father had said when we joined that he expected about six weeks' work would cure us of wanting a life on the land and my pride rebelled at proving him right.

Mrs Hope-Hannyngton had transferred our papers to Hampshire

when we returned to Bournemouth. We heard from Hampshire County Organiser on 5th October that she had accepted Cara's resignation, and that she could offer me temporary work – potato picking at the County Farm Institute farm at Sparsholt, near Winchester. Transport from Winchester to the Institute would be arranged from the County Offices on 7th October. I accepted the offer until something more permanent offered and before I lost my nerve to carry on alone.

Those precious home leaves.

After a rather restless night, on Monday I packed up once more, and was glad of the company of Mother and Cara as far as Winchester. We enjoyed a browse round the city before lunching together at the Cadena and going to the WLA County Headquarters to look for the promised transport. I was reassured to find three other Land Girls waiting, though they looked no more cheerful than I felt. We were helped to climb into the back of a large lorry by the cheerful driver. Sitting on hard benches down the sides of the lorry, the sight of Cara returning to the station with Mother sent my heart sinking right down into my tough Land Army boots. The four of us Land Girls struck up a desultory conversation during the jolty ride and admired the country views we drove through for about four miles. About a mile after the village of Sparsholt we drew up outside an imposing large hostel building at the top of a rise with a commanding view of gardens and farm buildings, set in attractive undulating country. It had an impersonal feel after our family farm life and I suddenly felt very alone.

5 Sparsholt Farm Institute

October - November 1940

AS WE CLIMBED THE FEW steps to the front entrance of Sparsholt Farm Institute we were greeted by the Warden, Miss Campion, and her rather older assistant, Miss Sylvester. Miss Sylvester then took us to our dormitory and showed us our common room. I was glad to see the dormitory was divided into cubicles, each offering a narrow camp bed, a chest of drawers and a wardrobe. We were told we were to keep the cubicles tidy, and swept and dusted. We would be expected on the farm at 7 am. Breakfast would be at 8 and we would have three-quarters of an hour for this, giving us time to make beds, etc. Lunch at noon allowed us an hour off; we would have our evening meal at 6 pm and a late drink and biscuit at 9. All girls *must* be in by 10 o'clock or would be locked out; they would have to disturb the Matron if later and would be in trouble.

It felt like boarding school all over again, and I was assailed by the homesickness that I had hoped was over once and for all when I so joyfully had left school. We went down to tea together, and I learned that my new companions were Nell Corner, Josie and Winnie. After tea we strolled round the grounds and put our coats and gumboots into the cloakroom beneath the hostel down a flight of stone steps beside the front door. (This cloakroom doubled as air-raid shelter at night, and jolly chilly it proved to be.)

After a session of writing letters home we had supper and then settled ourselves for an early night. I was cheered to find good bathroom accommodation, plenty of hot water for baths and lots of washbasins. How I wished Cara could have enjoyed this luxury accommodation with me. A far cry from our jug of cold water and bedroom basin at Bishops Frome. I rolled into my camp bed thinking of Cara still at home, and feeling great sympathy for Bill, away from home and his wife.

I had a restless night and slept only fitfully, feeling nervous and depressed, but felt better when 6 am at last came and I could get up and set out for some work. On our way to the cart-shed, where we were to meet the Farm Manager, we met Beryl and Mrs Bartram – Land Girls who had arrived before us, who were also on general farm work. The farm manager, Mr Ashenden, set us to work in the food loft over the barn, bagging up artificial manure until breakfast time. At 9 am, when we returned to the farm, we were sent off to the fields to clump couch grass; it rained all morning until we were drenched and feeling fed up.

Sparsholt Farm Institute.

After drying out and getting changed in the lunch hour, the afternoon was enjoyable, as I was potato picking and partnering the farm manager. He was very pleasant to work with, and I learnt quite a lot about the role of the Farm Institute. It had been suggested to me at school that I would enjoy training at this very college, so it seemed I was meant to be there. At 5 pm we knocked off and, before tea, indulged in hot baths to soothe our aching backs. After more letter writing home I went with Josie to the village. There was an air raid some way away – probably over Southampton – and we saw the exhaust of the enemy aircraft and the shells exploding round the planes; we said a prayer for all those involved.

The weather turned unpleasantly cold, wet and windy on Wednesday and Thursday. We were glad to finish bagging up the rest of the 87 cwt of potash, and pleased that we were getting better at handling weighty sacks. The potato picking for the rest of the day was hard going as I had a beastly headache. Though the farm foreman, Michael Greenhill, kept us hard at it, the day seemed long, though we liked this cheerful, good-looking bachelor. Some couch grass raking came as a restful change for our aching backs.

Michael Greenhill.

On Friday we were back to potato picking and Greenhill kept us hard at it. It was a lovely sunny day, we worked with a will and time went quickly. On our way back to the farm at the end of the day we met Mr Ashenden who cheered us by telling us to go to the farm office for our pay. For just four days' work I was paid sixteen shillings and a halfpenny. I looked forward to going shopping the next day, as we worked only a half day on Saturdays. I spent the evening writing a cheerful letter home, giving a more favourable account of life at the Farm Institute.

A friendly smile from Mr Ashenden was a good start when I arrived at the cart shed for the day's orders. On a bright and sunny morning Beryl and I were delighted to be taken off by Mr Greenhill to help him with renewing pig fencing. We held posts as he swung the mallet and tried to help pull the wires taut. It was an easy morning's work and Greenhill was chatty and had a great sense of humour. The other girls were quite envious when, over lunch, we recounted our morning's activity. We all went off by bus to Winchester and I made for WLA HQ to buy more secondhand uniform. A nearly-new pair of breeches cost me five shillings, a second pair of shoes was six shillings and sixpence, a very good shirt was only one shilling. I met Nell and Beryl at the Cadena for tea and by then we were all spent up and had an hour to wait for a Sparsholt bus. After a brief time in the common room, we were given coffee, bread and a biscuit for supper. We were ready for bed after listening to the 9 o'clock news and settled for sleep by 10, well content with our first week of the Farm Institute.

Sunday was a free day so I had a leisurely bath, got my room better organised and got my washing done before being summoned by the breakfast gong. Mrs Bartram, Joyce and Beryl then came to my room, and we decided to attend the morning service at the village church. Miss Campion and Miss Sylvester joined us there, and the Vicar and congregation were friendly and welcoming.

In the afternoon Beryl and I walked across the fields to the outdoor milking bail as Joyce was working there helping Mr Parsons with the milking. This bail was a sort of corrugated hut on wheels with stalls for four cows at a time. While the two machines milked two cows another two were being washed or having the last drops of milk stripped out. Food appropriate to the milk yields was released by a lever into the troughs. The herd milled around outside loose railings set up round the bail, awaiting their turn, a bull amongst them impatient for food he got at the end of milking. We kept a wary eye on him. The milk float grey horse, Dapple, was used to draw the

The Outdoor Milking Bail.

bail hut to clean ground after each milking, so there was no shed cleaning. Maybe this outdoor bail was an economy system for a small herd but not very comfortable, I would think, in cold wet weather. Joyce had the added job of unharnessing, grooming and feeding Dapple before coming in to tea. I decided I preferred cowshed milking.

The dull, cold, wet days of October did rather test our love of working on the land. Arriving back at the hostel in the evening, wringing wet, only to find tepid bathwater and that others had got in before us, offered little cheer.

The morning that Michael Greenhill said he wanted us first to unload the sacks of potatoes from a trailer and carry them up a ladder to the loft over the granary had us all laughing. We really thought it was his idea of a joke. He somewhat testily reminded us we were employed to replace farm men and that involved doing men's work. He patiently showed us how to drag the sacks to the edge of the trailer, and to get them really high on our shoulder. Sure enough, he had us up and down the ladder and we cleared a ton or two of potatoes from the trailer up into the loft. It gave us quite a sense of achievement, but we hoped not to have to do it too often. Potato sacks in the field were heavy enough to drag across muddy fields when wet, without having to negotiate ladders. I saw the lorry driver fall off that ladder one day, when carrying a sack, and he broke his collarbone. After that I always made sure a sack on my back was well-balanced.

If a wet potato harvest is hard work, harvesting sugar beet in wet muddy fields is even worse. Banging roots together did not get rid of much mud, and knives tended to slip when trying to make a neat job of chopping off the leaves. Throwing up the clumps of roots on to a trailer was a backbreaking job. Nell and I were thankful we were allowed to work the horses. I soon became practised at getting Pat, a quiet Shire, harnessed and into the shafts, but Nell was quicker with

Ploughing with Shires.

Punch, a lively Suffolk Punch, as she had the advantage of being tall. I had to run from side to side while she could reach over the horse's back. We enjoyed the ride to the field and I loved it when leading these gentle giants, and the feel of their soft lips and tickly moustaches against my hand. Jingling harness and the smell of horse sweat still evoke happy memories for me.

When we could not work on the sugar beet harvest, we helped Taffy (Trevor Anthony) with the pigs. I loved the pigs, and Nell grew to love Taffy. It was no surprise to me when they left the farm together and soon after sent me a slice of their wedding cake. My last letter from Nell was to report the arrival of their daughter. Joyce and I had become good friends, and we hoped we might be offered work together on our next farm. With this hope in mind, Joyce and I each turned down other jobs offered, though mine was to work horses on the farm of a Mrs Little. Joyce was invited to a general farm in Gloucester, but her father was very ill and she wanted to remain near her Surrey home.

Mr Ashenden, having told us he did not want Land Girls as permanent staff, as Sparsholt was to have trainee Land Girls coming every month shortly, suddenly relented. If we were willing to start work every morning, including Sundays at 5 am, he agreed to let Joyce stay to help Mr Parsons on the milking bail while I could help in the cowsheds. We accepted joyfully. We were to have Friday afternoon as our time off and we were to have a pay rise to thirty-five shillings a week.

We were thrilled – the conditions at Sparsholt were so good compared with some we had experienced on farms. Miss Campion, the Warden, congratulated us and said we would in future feed at the top table in the dining hall, as members of staff, and we could soon have the use of the comfortable library in the evenings as our common room. It was all very exciting, though I was a little regretful that working with Greenhill would now end, but I hoped I could still play with his beagle pups when he gave them their evening feed, as this had recently become a daily routine.

6 Cowshed Assistant

November 1940 - October 1941

EARLY IN NOVEMBER I FINISHED on general farm work. After lunch I went to the cowshed and after friendly greetings from Jack Lawley, my new boss, and Lofty, a farmhand helping out Jack until I could take over, I was sent to bring in a few Guernseys from a nearby field while Lofty fetched the main Shorthorn herd numbering about thirty pedigree cows. The milking was not as straightforward as I had expected – four different milking machines were in use and the cows always had to be milked by the same machine. This was to give college students experience with the different types of machines. Food had to be measured according to the yield of each cow. All the milk had to be weighed and recorded on a sheet against each cow's name. In between grooming tails and washing udders and stripping the last drops of milk from udders after removing the machines, I was madly making notes to help me cope at the next morning's milking. It was all a bit of a nightmare. I liked Jack very much however, and as it was evident he loved his cows, I felt we would get on well when I knew my job and could be a real help. I was glad to be working with animals again and it was quite cosy working under cover after our cold, rainy days in the beet field.

Working with Jack Lawley was very enjoyable as he was always cheerful and kindly and often sang as we milked. I shared his love of the cows and appreciated their distinct personalities. They were pets to us, and we shared the sorrow of losing any one of them, or their adorable new calves who often went for slaughter when very young, so that humans could benefit from their mothers' milk. The suffering of the bereaved cows was an added torture, but I hoped there was another life for calf martyrs. I rationalised that if there was

32

no slaughter of animals for food, there would be few farmers, and domestic animals rarely seen except in zoos. So much of farm produce was grown for animals and farming was a great life despite periods of rough weather.

On the rare occasions when I overslept I was never reproached by Jack, as I struggled to get accustomed to the 4.30 am alarm after a day of physical outdoor work. Joyce told me not to have the alarm clock within reach of the bed, so that I had to leap out to avoid disturbing the whole dormitory. This was a help and, once awake, we each checked to make sure the other was up. Outside, the air-raids in the Southampton area prevented the use of torches, which meant stumbling around dark fields, sometimes falling over sleeping cows, both to their discomfort and mine. In the process, I gained a life-long appreciation of that stillness and freshness of early pre-dawn, before the world returns to busy activity.

I found the searchlights a help some days, but it was worrying to see a red glow over the coast in the Southampton area, signifying another night of terror and destruction. Bournemouth did not escape bombs at that time, as enemy planes being chased out to sea by the gallant 'Few' would unload bombs to gain speed, via Bournemouth, to avoid the anti-aircraft guns bristling round the port. Evening phone calls home were frequent to check all was well after those noisy nights. The farm staff spent much time on night duty keeping an eye on the farm stock, scattered in surrounding fields, as well as taking turns as Home Guard volunteers and air-raid wardens in the village. Though it was sad to read of the death of Neville Chamberlain, I felt glad for him that he was out of this troubled world. He died on 9th November, as I was starting work with Jack.

When Joyce and I went into the common room that evening to play table tennis and darts, the Warden, Miss Campion, came to tell us that in future we had the use of the very nice library room in the evenings. It had comfortable chairs, plenty of technical books on farming and a large table for writing or studying. We could hardly believe our good fortune in having such ideal living conditions.

During November Jack had a morning off to register for call-up, though he was unlikely to be taken off his farm work. He also had time off with lumbago. At these times and on his day off, Chris, a general farm worker, used to help in the sheds. Chris was no lover of cows nor of cowshed work, so everything was done at great speed and the cows were nervous at the rough treatment meted out. I did not appreciate these times any more than the cows, but it meant I was in the hostel in good time for the evening meal.

There was a bit of excitement when the Minister of Agriculture came to visit the Institute and to lunch with the Principal, Mr Smith. As this was a Friday and Joyce and I were going to Winchester for our afternoon off, we excused ourselves to go and catch the bus. On our return, Miss Campion informed us that thirty-five Whitehall officials were to pay the Institute a visit and our dormitory would be needed for a night or two from 3rd December. Between the 2nd and 4th December we slept in the air-raid shelter, and were glad to do so, as the hostel reeked of cigarette and pipe smoke. On Wednesday 4th, Mr Smith requested that the cowshed be cleaned by 9.15 am as he would be bringing the officials to look round. As the cows were now being bedded down at night in the shed, on deep straw, and being hay fed before being turned out, we managed to achieve this but not without difficulty, nor too happily.

When Joyce and I got in to breakfast we found ourselves surrounded by twenty-two of the visitors. Though Greenhill was not there his beagle, Radiant, was, and the Ministers were feeding her from the table and giving her coffee to drink. This would not please Michael, I knew, so when she started to run about in the hostel, which was not permitted, I managed to catch her and get her back to the farm. I returned to the hostel and found a parcel from home in which was a letter from Mother, arranging to meet Joyce and me for tea in Winchester the next day. I was so excited the hours fairly dragged for the rest of the day. Now the visitors had left, I spent the evening taking my possessions back to our dormitory.

Try as we might the next day to get the work done quickly in order to finish early, we were both late for lunch and had a mad rush to catch the one o'clock bus. At 2 pm we had met up with Mother and Flo (an Irish friend of Cara's, now living with the family). It was a lovely afternoon, catching up on home news, and we were sad when we had to part company at 5 o'clock, hoping they would avoid air-raids in Southampton on their train ride home. The day ended cheerfully when Greenhill brought some of his records into the library and spent the evening with us.

The work in December was tough going – having to carry straw throughout the cowshed each evening and fill the racks with hay, and seeing that the cows were secure and comfortable for the night after milking often made me late for the evening meal. The morning was almost completely taken up in making the shed tidy and clean for milking and, following the milking, getting the cows out. After breakfast we had to clear out all the straw before we could wash down the shed. The loose boxes also had more stock kept in at night, so took longer to clean out. Rations for the cows were increased, so there was a lot of cake mixing to do. Being busy made the days fly and we were sad that Christmas meant no holiday for us. We were told we could have a night at home some time in January, but that did not have the same feel, though we rejoiced that we could get home then.

One day just before Christmas I opened the *Bournemouth Times* (sent to me by Dad each week) to read that Philip Anstey, an R.A.F. Sgt. Observer, was reported missing after a raid. Philip's father was manager of our local branch of W.H. Smith, and we had often joined in beach games with Philip and his friends. He was very popular with all the young set. There was I feeling sad about missing Christmas at home, but how much anxiety and misery the Anstey family must suffer.

Christmas Eve was rainy and mild and, though the morning went well, I had Chris racing through the milking in the afternoon, and was glad to get finished. We were in good time for the evening meal, and I went off to have a good bath and think of days long gone when, as little ones in Tredegar, we would have been sent early to bed, and used to climb the stairs excitedly singing 'Jingle Bells', with dreams of what Father Christmas might bring – such happy, family days, days of such security. Just as well we had not known then of the war to come. I was wondering how Cara and Bill were to spend Christmas when Miss Campion knocked on the door to tell me that Captain Anderson, the College Bursar, had offered to drive us into Winchester to see a good film. We were ready in a flash. Captain Anderson said he could not stay for the film, but that there would be a taxi waiting outside the cinema to take us back to the hostel. What a good friend to sense we needed a bit of cheering up on our first Christmas away from our families. It was an enjoyable evening, rounded off by being invited into Miss Campion's room to enjoy a feast of mince pies with Captain Anderson and his mother. We did appreciate this kindness and thoughtfulness.

Mr. Ashenden,
Farm Manager

Christmas Day was happier than I could have imagined. Not only did Jack and I let rip, singing every Christmas carol known to us as we worked, but the general farmhands turned up to help us speedily through the clearing up. Lunchtime saw a gathering of all the farm hands, in the dining hall, and we had a very enjoyable traditional Christmas dinner together. I felt honoured to find myself placed next to Mr Ashenden who added much to my enjoyment, with his great sense ol humour and fun.

I was only sad that Jack and I had to leave the party to return to our cows, just as the folk were lining up to dance the Roger de Coverley as a start to the Christmas dance. Some of the men, not wanting to join the dancing after so ample a meal, came with us and gave a hand to help us get a long evening off. I found more good company in the hostel, including the Principal, his family and Billy, a lively and amusing cockney evacuee. We were joined by Miss Campion, Captain Anderson and the Captain's mother. I was quite sorry when supper interrupted the evening and I retired with Joyce to the library, where we enjoyed listening to records until late. A wonderful Christmas, indeed.

As 1940 came to its close, Joyce, Nell, and I decided we would retire early to bed, and not see in the New Year, since we had to be up so early. As I lay in bed I thought over the changes 1940 had brought in my life. January 1940 seemed so remote, a time when I was at home and the war seemed unreal. Ration books were about to be issued but the war had hardly affected us, though we read of the dreadful hardships of troops in Europe in Arctic weather, and we were having very wintry conditions.

Cara was working in London, but frequently returned home at weekends. Bill was studying for his law finals, Jill was at school, and I was about to start work at Boscombe Hospital. The fall of France and the Dunkirk evacuation really woke us up to our serious involvement in war. Though it never for a moment entered our heads that we might possibly lose the war, it did urge us into a more active role in the defence of our country. Suddenly our world had been turned upside down, families scattered and bereaved and the nations, who all presumably preferred to live in peace, were locked in this crazy combat. The chug-chug of distant enemy planes lulled me to sleep feeling there was now little prospect of an early restoration of peace and sanity in this mad world.

The Institute had undertaken the training of young men with a conscientious objection to being involved in military activity. While respecting their moral courage in sticking to their principles, we did not feel any obligation to spend time with them after working hours, while so many young lives were gallantly given in defence of our country and in striving to rescue Europe from Hitler; we felt the greater loyalty to the fighting forces.

With the influx of 'conchies' and batches of Land Girls arriving each month, the atmosphere in the hostel and on the farm quickly changed, and we found it quite unsettling for a time. In the hostel we were told that, in future, we were to share our meals with the Land Girls, but we could retain the use of the library in the evenings. We were grateful for this concession, as the shouting and singing, the tramping of heavy boots and the cigarette smoke made the hostel a very different environment from the quiet and orderly home we had grown accustomed to.

On the farm we were having to help to train the girls in the more mundane work, so saw less of the farm staff. I was glad I was still invited to help Greenhill in the evening with his dogs. He had season tickets for Winchester Concerts by the London Philharmonic Orchestra, conducted by Malcolm Sargent in the Town Hall, and I got occasional invitations to go to concerts with him. This was a great thrill, and we sometimes sat behind Ralph Richardson and Laurence Olivier, who were billeted at the nearby Fleet Air Arm station and looked great in uniform.

Despite the new circumstances in the hostel and on the farm, Jack and I continued to work happily in the cowsheds, and shared the sorrows of cows ill or old and having to go for slaughter. Pride, a beautiful and valuable Guernsey, became very ill after swallowing a long hair-clip while grazing. Watching that cow suffer for days taught me why farmers are sometimes reluctant to let the public use their fields for picnics and the like. Cows pull at grass with their tongues and readily pick up litter which can be a great danger to them. Not everyone realizes that grass is a valuable food crop for animal feed. Tiny, a great little cow character, grew too old and, as her milk yield was not up to scratch, off she went for slaughter, along with Jewel's new twins. I never became hardened to this side of farming, and sympathised with Jack not having any say in these matters. It was a management decision.

Jack (left) and Taffy with 'Crusader'.

Greenhill provided me with some lighter moments when he decided to write a book on farmcraft for WLA recruits . An artist friend of his, Evelyn Dunbar, undertook to help with illustrations. She sometimes asked me to pose with a milk pail or pitchfork to help with the sketches. She was a charming person so I enjoyed these sessions and being allowed this small role in the publication.

After I had worked with Jack for six months, I was asked by Mr Ashenden if I thought I could manage the afternoon milking work with the aid of Land Girls, so that Jack could have his day off. Chris had decided to leave farm work and join the Forces. I was somewhat apprehensive about taking this on, but knew Jack needed his after noon off, so I agreed to have a go. This was to prove quite a disastrous mistake. Jack suddenly became very critical of everything I did. When Joyce came into the shed to help, he butted in and separated us if we dared to exchange a few words. He behaved so oddly and so out of character that life became difficult. Jack's mother suddenly became very cool in her attitude towards me, and Joyce and I were

Overleaf: Illustrations from A Book of Farmcraft.

1

2

3

4

USE OF PITCHFORK

RIGHT

WRONG

USE OF BUSHEL MEASURE

RIGHT

WRONG

CARRYING A SACK

READY TO MILK

quite nonplussed, until one day Mr Parsons told Joyce that Jack had warned him that Joyce and I were scheming together to take over their jobs and we were not to be trusted, talking together.

I did not at once connect all this with me taking on Jack's work on his day off at Mr Ashenden's request and I was very hurt that Jack should have so wretched an opinion of me, as I had felt we were on such good terms. The atmosphere became so strained that I went to see Mr Ashenden about returning to doing general farm work, though I was very sad at the thought of leaving the cows. Mr Ashenden appeared irritated by Jack's change of attitude, but agreed I could be switched back to general farm work, as Taffy and Nell were also to leave the farm for work in Wales. I would have to continue helping Jack with the milking for some time yet, but I could do general farm work between the milkings. This eased the situation with Jack somewhat, but he did not seem overpleased that shed cleaning and the like would now be done by trainees under his guidance. I worked with Greenhill a lot of the time and was allowed to do some tractor driving, haymaking and harvesting as the season wore on.

Miss Campion left to join the Red Cross, and was replaced by an older woman, Mrs Bruce. None of us appreciated the change, as the hostel rules and regulations became more than ever like a boarding school. As we were adults, and old enough to leave home to help with the war effort, we thought the regulations an unnecessary infringement on our liberty. Complaints to Mr Smith fell on rather unsympathetic ears. He felt rules and regulations could do us no harm.

We were joined on most outings by Betty Hunt who had been taken onto the staff and was likely to replace me in the cowshed, and I was to learn how to take charge of the considerable herd of pedigree large white pigs.

Happy though I was to be on general farm work much of the day the hours were very long during harvest, as I was still getting up for milking at 4.30 and having to work evenings in the fields until dusk when the weather was suitable. After supper I often took the horses to their field when they had eaten and cooled off to save the carter having to return two miles from his cottage. I enjoyed this, as I loved to watch them canter off for a roll when released, but they were quite a handful as they became excited as we got near their field. To prevent their great hoofs landing on my gumboots I would lift my feet off the ground and let them carry me, by hanging on to their halters. I was lucky to be in bed by 11 o'clock after this job. To be allowed to turn hay with horse and tedder, gave me a restful and enjoyable spell. Not so restful, but enjoyable, was a day of harrowing, once I had learnt to make the horses turn slowly, and not tangle up the harrows at the field end.

It was a relief when, at the end of October, I could say goodbye to my partnership with Jack in the cowsheds, and return to 7.30 am rising. We parted good friends again, as I was no longer considered a threat to Jack's job, and we exchanged small gifts and were both a bit sad at the parting.

7 Sparsholt Pig Lady
October 1941 - July 1942

HOW LOVELY IT WAS, WAKING up at 4.30, to hear Joyce and Betty getting up while I snuggled down for another two hours. At 7 I was greeted cheerily in the cart shed by Ashenden, and introduced to the Land Girls as the 'Pig Lady'. Greenhill then took me off to teach me this new role.

The pedigree large white herd consisted of about twenty breeding sows, some housed in pens around the farmyard and some with litters in a fairly remote field, in movable units. When the piglets were weaned and able to leave the sows, they were moved to Danish house. This Danish house was divided into pens each side of a centre gangway, so that pigs could be separated according to weight until achieving the right weight for market. Feeding was a simple matter of filling troughs from the gangway with buckets of meal and water. Cleaning the pens was simple, as pigs did not soil bedding but used a passage behind the pen. Doors to each pen across the passage would shut each pen while sweeping the passage right through and out of a door at the end.

Trainee Land Girls got into trouble with me when they tried to improve the cleaning job by spraying eau de cologne around. I soon learned how to mix rations, but hated loading up pigs for market. How pigs could scream when frightened, or when hungry! Each morning, as soon as I opened the door of Danish house, the noise could be heard for miles until every trough was being sucked dry. Then the screams were changed for contented 'slurpy' sounds as the pigs struggled against each other to get every scrap they could. One tiny runt was not satisfied with his rations and discovered he could slip through the bars over the troughs and make his escape if the

Danish house door was left open. His life was threatened when he was found, more than once, in the farm gardens, having a lovely feast. I decided the only answer was to take him around with me. He became a great pet, and went everywhere with me, on a halter. He was known to all as Henry, and made lots of friends. The farm manager was not too impressed – walking round with me did not add much to Henry's weight. Inevitably the sad day came when the blow fell. "Anne, you must take that runt round to the slaughterhouse. The hostel needs him for food." I pleaded with Ashenden in vain and was reminded there was a war, and we were working to produce food. I took poor Henry round, still on the halter, gave him a generous helping of food and knocked him out myself with the 'humane killer', then left the farm men to deal with him while I rushed off to feed the rest of the herd, so that I was not seen with tears streaming in mourning for my cheerful piggy friend. While the Hostel rejoiced at the delicious pork, bacon and sausage meals, I was happy to give my share to others at the table.

Inside the Danish house.

Though there was a lot to do for pigs, with preparing rations, cleaning out, fencing, and keeping an eye on farrowing sows, which can easily crush their newborn offspring inadvertently while attending to the newest arrival, and coping with the boars and matings, the job I liked best was dealing with the sows and litters in a distant field. These were kept in movable units, and involved taking food with horse and cart, and using the horse (taken out of the shafts) to move the units. I also had to take a water cart up at times, to supply their troughs. The piglets roamed freely, able to get in and out of the pens from openings too small for the sows. The sows would have churned up the field too much unless their snouts had rings put in to prevent this. When the piglets saw me coming, it was wonderful to see a great wave of them racing across the field, screaming for food all the way. At one time, this job became very hazardous, because a grazing young bull had broken his tether and, being of very uncertain temperament, none of the farm men were in any hurry to try to recapture 'Revels Crusader'. I had much too exciting a time in the meantime, dodging his attentions, while trying to get the pigs fed and watered.

Appeals to Jack met with, "Don't you worry Missie, Crusader is only young and he's just rather playful still". Playful, my foot! He would charge at me as soon as he saw me, and I had to dodge round and round the water cart many a day, and only by giving him lots of pig meal could I get the pigs dealt with. To my great delight, when being literally 'bullied', I saw the Principal enter the other end of the field with another man.

"Look Billy, men in your field," I told Crusader, and away he went at top speed.

Mr Smith and friend just made it to the gate in time. The very next day several farmhands were up there with Jack and Crusader was captured and reluctantly led away to a loose box to be tamed. Care of the unit pigs was a joy once more.

Greenhill was a good friend, often helping with pig management and occasionally taking me to the pictures, or for walks with the dogs. This helped a lot through the dull autumn months, as life in the hostel was not very enjoyable. We all talked about the possibility of looking for new work, though Betty seemed to be enjoying the cowshed work despite the early rising. Joyce felt she should be nearer her mother, and if Joyce left I would not want to stay on.

We were cheered to hear there would be some trainees at the farm over Christmas, so we could go home this year. My brother was to be on embarkation leave, so I was given a night at home earlier in December, to say farewell to Bill. Japan had now joined the conflict and prompted America in to help the Allies; there seemed no prospect of an early end to the war. Japan had already sunk two of our battleships off Malaya – the *Prince of Wales* and the *Repulse* – with great loss of life – there would be no mood of rejoicing for many at Christmas.

In the last week before Christmas Greenhill got us decorating the library with paper chains and holly to cheer us. The killing of a pig for the hostel Christmas fare was not so cheering for me, but at least I would not be involved in the feasting, as I would be with the family.

Just my luck that my sow, Clip 5, decided to start farrowing as I was about to leave for Bournemouth on Christmas Eve, but Greenhill took over and I caught my train. I had left everything as tidy and organised as I could, and was told later that Mr Smith had said that he was pleased that Miss Hall had "got the pigs up together and in good order". That was very encouraging, as I had tried to keep them

Boar amongst Gilts.

all looking well cared for. I really enjoyed this work and I could tell one pig family from another. To most people all pigs look alike, but through working with them constantly I could see family likenesses.

To be back with my family, and at home, was a wonderful tonic. I was reluctant to go to bed so sat listening to the wireless until midnight. Churchill and Roosevelt broadcast a Christmas message from America and sang carols. Despite the late night I was first to wake and roused Cara when examining presents that had arrived on my bed. We decided to go to the early service at St. Saviour's, and Dad joined us. The side chapel only was lit and already full, so we sat behind in the dark church. A lovely, peaceful and meaningful start to the day, exchanging greetings with friends from my former life. My sister Jill wanted to attend a service, so I went again with her to matins. We enjoyed a good sing of carols, then returned to a traditional lunch, and wondered what Alan and Bill would have to eat to celebrate in their Army quarters. We lunched with Aunt Gwen and Granny; after listening to the King's speech, and the traditional walk with the dog on the cliffs, we returned home. Boxing Day gave me a chance to catch up on Cara's news of college days over coffee in Bournemouth after a walk along the promenade, which was soon to be closed to the public. All too soon 3.30 pm and the train to Winchester saw me being torn reluctantly from home once more, though I had so enjoyed the brief break.

I worked with pigs till the end of July. In those months I was taught a lot by Greenhill, who helped me to mix the right foods, to assess the probable weight of the pigs and decide when to weigh them to check whether they were ready to be 'notified' and to go to market. I was given their pedigrees to study and taught how to manage the breeding sows and the boars known as 'Nook' and 'Beau'. I was shown how to castrate the baby pigs, how to impress the litter number in the ears and how to clip tiny nicks round the ears to match their mothers' 'clips' (hence their family names, 'clip 5', 'clip 20', etc.). I would have to parade young gilts or boars before farmers wanting new stock. Most of the time, however, was spent on the daily routine of feeding and cleaning and mixing new rations, with the aid of trainees.

Moving pigs from one pen to another round the farm could be very time-consuming as the pigs would rush in all directions, so Greenhill always helped with these operations. Pigs who got into the gardens, snatching at vegetables as they ran, would land us in serious trouble.

When Greenhill had the tractor near the field of outdoor units, he would move the units with the tractor and save me a lot of time. I used to enjoy riding Pat, a shire horse, up to the units to bring the water cart back to the farmyard for a refill – as having returned it to the field I could ride Pat back and enjoy the wide views.

Michael Greenhill teaching tractor driving.

The winter of 1942 was very dismal. Not only was the war news increasingly depressing, but the weather seemed viciously cold and, even in the hostel, we sat by the radiators and felt we were keeping them warm, rather than the other way round. The winds were arctic, and a good layer of snow made the carrying of heavy buckets of swill very hard for me as, being short, they dragged on the snow. Try as I might to reach their troughs before they reached me, I quite often got rolled in the snow by the charge of my very large sows as they raced to me across a paddock, all attempting to be first to the food. I always had one trough more than there were pigs in a paddock. They bullied one another out of their trough, so having a spare one ensured all could keep racing from trough to trough, yet always have one each. The weather made them desperate for their food.

Not only did I get very tired in those dark winter days but the arrival of another Land Girl, Judy, a very pleasant blonde and a good worker, meant that she became of great interest to Greenhill. The evening invitations out were more often Judy's than mine. Betty had become friendly with the Ashendens, and so Judy and Michael were often out with Betty and the Ashendens in the evening. Though Greenhill and I remained as friendly at work I quite missed his company, feeding his dogs and walking together many an evening.

It seemed a never-ending January for all of us, and there was a near riot in the hostel when Mrs Bruce decided the resident Land Girls should do their own washing up. We complained to Mr Smith and threatened to see our WLA Rep. and he told Mrs Bruce we were not to be given domestic duties. This did not improve the hostel atmosphere, and Joyce and I looked at advertisements in the farming papers, deciding it was time we had a change. A new tutor in the dairy, Joy Gane, arrived on the scene like a breath of fresh air. She was well-named Joy, being always full of the joys of spring (though it seemed a long time coming!). I was chided if I dared to say I was fed up and told to count my blessings, when others were so much worse off. Joy used to spend her evenings in the library with us, and was so energetic on the farm she always had time to give one of us a hand to get our work finished, and often got us going to concerts or films in Winchester, and cheered us on nicely.

Greenhill was a help. Realising I was getting rather worn down, he persuaded Ashenden I needed a break, and volunteered to do the pigs while I had a weekend off early in February. I was also given a rise to thirty-one shillings a week, and Joyce was given £2 on her bail job. This was a real encouragement, as we were always hard up. Joyce had a lot to be sad about at that time – her father was seriously ill and not expected to recover. She went home to give moral support to her mother, whenever she could be spared, as her brother was away in the Forces. When Joyce was at the farm we spent most of our time together. We both found great comfort in churchgoing. In February the Vicar of Sparsholt suddenly resigned, causing a lot of rumours about the reason for his going the day before Ash Wednesday. Army Chaplains from a nearby camp came to the rescue and one in particular, the Reverend Aylmer Cameron, was very helpful to us both in his preaching and coming in the early hours of a weekday to give us Communion when we were unable to get to the Sunday service on account of work. To do this, he not only had to use his personal petrol coupons for the drive but had to spend time putting up 'black-outs' in the church. He insisted that this was no trouble, and he was glad to do it. At that time, our faith needed just the boost his inspired preaching offered. We never forgot that Lent, when we felt we were helped to grow spiritually. (Forty years later I rediscovered the whereabouts of Aylmer Cameron, and was delighted to be able to write him a belated letter of thanks, after I had been able to help

At Sparsholt Church.

the faith of others with his teaching, when I became a vicar's wife and helped in the Ministry for thirty-five years.)

It was in February that Michael Greenhill one day made me a present of a copy of the newly-produced *Book of Farmcraft*. It was signed by Michael and the illustrator Evelyn Dunbar, with a little note of thanks for 'holding a pitchfork so patiently'. This gift gave me a great thrill as a memento of watching the production of that helpful guide to Land Girls, and I felt my thanks inadequate to express what it meant to me. (It is still treasured, but would make strange reading to prospective land workers of today.) I was glad to have this gift just then as I was having a weekend at home and could show it off and leave it there for safe keeping.

8 Restless For A Change
March - July 1942

ONCE MARCH WAS OVER THE weather grew warmer and the work less arduous. Twenty-three trainee Land Girls were a mixed blessing, but helpful on the farm on the whole. I envied Betty and Judy, often invited in the evening to play tennis with Ashenden and Greenhill.

I was beginning to feel less interest in full-time pig management so Joyce and I were wondering whether the time had come to look for work together on a private farm offering more variety of work. I felt both Greenhill and Ashenden were less pleased with my efforts, though I was not conscious of easing off. Greenhill's spare time was more often spent with Judy and Ashenden was more quick to find fault with my work, so maybe it was time for a change. Betty and Joy Gane, surprisingly, were also saying they thought perhaps it was time for a move. Life in the hostel had never been as enjoyable without Miss Campion in charge and with the trainees swarming around what had once been our nice quiet quarters. Perhaps it was simply the arrival of spring stirring us up.

The arrival of the threshing machine at the farm meant the withdrawal of my trainees, so I had to do the pig management alone. Greenhill developed 'flu' just as Ashenden was sufficiently recovered to take a holiday. Without much top management the farm took on a rather relaxed air, until Greenhill returned and took charge in the absence of Ashenden. I was not conscious of having taken things easy but Greenhill came into the Danish house and gave me a lecture about my having slackened off. The bolts on the door of the pig pens had not been kept greased; the windows of the Danish House were a disgrace; the rails over the feed troughs were in desperate need of a wash down. Where was my early enthusiasm for the work? Not a question I could easily answer except that it seemed a jolly long war set to be much longer yet. I had to admit all these jobs needed attention though I doubted this had caused any harm to the pigs. When Ashenden returned and also gave me a lecture suggesting my efforts were not good enough, I thought he was blaming me for the amount of newborn piglets lost during a bad winter. It convinced me they wanted to replace me and I must get on with finding another job.

In June, Greenhill told me he had accepted a job on a large Sussex estate. This really decided me I would leave. Though I had felt fed up with Greenhill and his criticisms, I suddenly realized that Sparsholt for me would not be the same without him. He had been a good friend and I would miss his presence and help in many ways. I decided to advertise for a job, though Joyce felt this was asking for unsatisfactory employers to be the most likely to offer work, as they could be reluctant to be known to be always advertising for more workers. To get things moving I was game to take this risk – I hoped I would have a choice of jobs to decide on.

Calling on some neighbours to tell them I was going to look for other work, and perhaps hoping for concern or disappointment, I was upset to be told, "A right decision my dear. Mr Smith and Mr Ashenden have been very displeased with your work for some months." If so, why not tell me to go? I returned to the hostel fuming, feeling bitter and hating everyone. I still could not see where I had failed them all so badly, but at least it made leaving a place where I had been so happy a lot easier.

Dad readily agreed to send a suitable advertisement to the farming papers, with my home address. He would forward any replies with his comments if I would find that helpful. I agreed that I would like him to do that. The phone call home calmed my mood and I determined to work like mad, get the pig work well up to scratch and make time to do quite a bit of general work as well, if possible. The sting of the unexpected criticism gave me a new rush of energy, and I really enjoyed the next few weeks. I did some carting of hay and straw, and taught trainees how to harness and handle the horses. I discovered heifers in the hay field and, as I set to work with a trainee to drive them out, Ashenden came to help and seemed to appreciate my efforts. He then asked me to go and collect hay rakings – though I was already behind with pig work, I thought it wise not to protest. The next morning I was able to alert the carter, at home, that I had just seen all six horses – Pat, Punch, Flower, Violet, Alec and Mose – trotting off to the village, presumably having found a gap in a hedge, or a gate left open. Carter Stanley Diment soon appeared at the farm driving the horses back. I was roped in later by Fred to sharpen knives as he mowed oats and vetches. He had spare knives and I was kept busy working with a metal file to have a sharp knife ready for the mower each time he returned to my end of the field.

Stan Diment driving Shires.

I received seventeen replies to the advertisement, and after a pleasant and satisfactory interview at Clanville, with Captain Heath, I accepted his offer of a job. When I told Mr Ashenden I should be leaving in ten days' time he seemed quite concerned and said he wished he had known I wanted to leave. He wanted to know where I was going to work and said he would have liked to make discreet enquiries about the work and my future employer before I had accepted the job, and that I was to contact him if I had any problems. He gave no indication of his relief that I was leaving, for which I was grateful. He did give me a good reference in case I needed one in the future. I asked if I might spend some time with the cows to brush up my hand milking, as Captain Heath would not use machines on his valuable pedigree herd of Shorthorns. I was told I could be useful on bail and in the sheds, as Betty was on leave and Joyce on compassionate leave.

I greatly enjoyed being in the shed with Jack during the afternoons; we were good friends once more and he was being helped by the dairy tutors – Joy Gane and Miss Archer – who were very speedy and efficient, and great fun. I still coped with my pigs and went to the bail for morning milkings. As soon as Gwen heard I was leaving and Joyce going very shortly, she gave in her notice, leaving Betty feeling she should go too. It was quite sad contemplating the break-up of our fun together.

One day, while helping to clean the cowsheds after milking, Joy came charging in and said, "Come on! Hurry, we are getting a lift to the flicks in Mr Batty's van". I was rushed away to get changed and clambered into the van to find Gwen and Joy already there. Mr Batty raced along to the Odeon with us, and in the queue were Mr and Mrs Ashenden, Judy, and a new Land Army recruit to the staff, Kay Eperon (the former ballet dancer). Only then did I realise this was a way of making my farewell memorable. The film was 'How Green Was My Valley'. (Yes, despite the ups and downs, I was now made to realize how green was my Sparsholt 'Valley'.) Mr Batty and I did not come out with eyes red and swollen, but almost everyone else did. Tears were never far away during the war and that was one of the saddest films. Hearing all the sniffing and seeing all the eye wiping, on this evening of entertainment, struck me as being a funny way to enjoy oneself, though it was a very good film about Wales in the depression years, a time and place I vaguely remembered from childhood days when we lived in Tredegar.

Arriving back at the hostel I was dragged off to the dairy, though it was after 10.30. The dairy had been thoroughly blacked out, and was well lit when we were all safely inside. There on a beautifully decked table was a lavish feast. This had all been done in great secrecy in honour of my departure. Mr Ashenden sat opposite me. He made a short speech of thanks to me for my contribution to the farm life of the Institute and for help with trainees. He presented me with a lovely table lamp and the others then sang, 'For She's a Jolly Good Fellow'. This really did bring tears to my eyes. Then came the feasting. It was an astonishing peace-time spread of meat sandwiches, cakes and biscuits, all home-baked, and lashings of fruit and dairy cream. I was so surprised and overwhelmed, I did not know how to thank them, but I think they knew how I felt. It was an evening I never forgot, and made leaving all those good friends very much more difficult.

I did my last morning's work at the Institute the next day, and at noon had a cup of tea with Miss Archer, Joy, and Mr Batty in the dairy and was able to thank them again for so enjoyable an evening and all the trouble they had gone to to arrange such a feast. I was sad to say goodbye to Mr Ashenden after he had been such a good employer for two years, and I left Sparsholt Farm Institute with a heavy heart, but with some wonderful memories and friends.

9 Clanville Lodge

August 1942 - June 1943

I WAS LOOKING FORWARD TO a week at home as I was very tired. I was delighted to hear from Captain Heath, my new employer; I was to start work in two weeks' time, on 10th August. It made me feel it had been worth changing my job to get two whole weeks of home life. At home, the activity at night over Bournemouth gave us no sleepless nights as it was mostly the drone of our aircraft setting off for raids over Germany. The days were quiet too, spent with family and friends, catching up on news and views.

My sister-in-law, Enid, called in frequently frustrated at still having no address for Bill, who had reached his unknown destination and was said to be travelling overland to his base, somewhere in the world. Enid was longing to pass on the news that they were to be parents in March, all being well. Cousin Alan, who was in the Gunners, was in camp on Salisbury Plain awaiting an overseas posting. It was lovely that he managed a forty-eight hour leave while I was still home.

On 10th August, Mother decided to travel with me to Andover, to visit her former headmistress, who had also helped Cara and me with school work when we were young. I went with Mother to see Miss Page, and was told to use her home as a 'home from home' when I was given any time off. This I was always glad to do, and enjoyed many meals at her home, 'The Nook'.

Having seen Mother on the Bournemouth bus after tea with Miss Page and her companion Miss Hanson, I got a bus to Clanville and went to see Captain Heath at the Lodge. After a rather formal welcome I was not thrilled to be told I was not having digs in the farm cottage in the farmyard opposite the dairy. Instead, I was to stay with an RAF family in the village. I was shown a path through a copse

Top: Clanville Lodge Billet;
Bottom Left: Thea Mathews and
daughters, Zella, Myrna and Lois;
Bottom right: Tom Mathews
in his new R.A.F. uniform.

near the house which I had previously been told were to be my digs. This path led to the side of the cottages where I was now expected.

Tom and Thea Mathews had three little girls – Zella, Myrna, and Lois. They had a dog, Peter, and a cat, Tim. This family gave me a very warm welcome; Tom at once relieved me of my luggage and took me up an enclosed staircase leading from their one living room. The bedroom was very roomy; it had nice beams and chintzy curtains – a pleasant character cottage room though somewhat chilly, and with small windows not offering much light. Tom told me he was working at Andover Air Force Station and, though often able to spend nights at home, Thea would be very glad of my company when he was away on 'ops'. I was interested that he dealt with photography, not a role I had thought of as an R.A.F. occupation.

The cottage was thatched, one of a terrace row, opposite the Red Lion pub. It was perhaps fairly typical of farm workers' cottages of that day, but was a new experience to me. It offered no mains services – no gas, electricity or water, no bathroom, no indoor sanitation. There was neither wash basin nor kitchen sink. As I was to be first up the next day I was taken to the end of the cottage row to be shown the well, and I was given a go at dropping the bucket to demonstrate what a lot of handle turning was needed to bring up each pail of water. Thea Mathews said they would usually fill three buckets at each visit to the well. I would need to use the primus stove to make myself an early cup of tea. Washing up was done in a basin on the kitchen table, the used water thrown on the garden. There was a garden hut down the side path in the back garden which housed an Elsan bucket loo.

The job of a daily dig in the garden for disposal of bucket contents was attended to by Tom, but when he was away in the Air Force, Thea would be grateful for my help with this, as she was not very good at digging. (After a few months of this walk down the garden in all weathers I never cease to appreciate home comforts and a chain to pull.) I got used to the evening glow of an oil lamp, and candles and torches, and enjoyed life with that kind family despite the primitive conditions.

By the side of the cottages was the path which was a shortcut to the farm, but it led through a small copse which I found quite creepy in the dark, as there were always owls hooting rather dismally during the dark evenings. I used to go with all speed through that wood.

My first night I was restless as there was much scuttering in the thatch overhead and I kept looking at the time. I got up at 5.30 and braved the cold water wash, went down quietly and managed to make myself a cup of tea, and took one to Thea and Tom before setting off to the farm. The cows were in the shed and Smeeton, the farm manager, introduced me to Miss Knight, friend of the Heaths, who helped on the farm. I enjoyed the milking session but the cows were reluctant to part with their milk to a stranger. After breakfast the Captain helped me to clean sheds, loose boxes and calf pens. He was particular about them being done well, as he took great pride in his valuable herd.

I was delighted when he brought me letters from Michael Greenhill and Betty. Michael was enjoying working on an Earl De La Warr estate. I was sad to hear from Betty that Joyce's father had died. I worked with a Land Girl, Peggy (also a new employee), who lived in the cottage adjoining the Mathews', with Mr Tubb, the farm carter, and his wife. Peggy was very unhappy about our primitive cottage digs, and intended to see the local Rep. to complain about them. I was not unduly bothered as I was ready to go off to bed soon after I got in, and one could not do much by the light of the one oil lamp the children had on the table for doing their homework. Peggy missed town life, as few buses ran into Andover in the evening. We enjoyed hoeing together as we compared our farm experiences. I liked helping Smeeton when he was rick thatching and I did the 'yelming' – making tidy straw bundles to hand up to him for the thatch.

When Smeeton and farmhand Tubbs set to work scything a path round the six-acre field of wheat, Peggy and I were set to tying the loose corn into sheaves, bound with a few corn stalks. The cutter and binder started work after tea and Smeeton and I were busy stooking until the light went. The Captain, Lady Marjorie, Miss Elizabeth, Master Andrew and Miss Knight worked with us for a time. The corn harvest kept us busy until Saturday. After a longer lunch-hour I milked five cows and was free after doing the dairy work, so I went off to 'The Nook' for the evening, and was treated to a good meal and a happy evening.

I was very glad Miss Page lived near enough for me to cycle to her home when I had a spare hour or two, as I quickly learnt that time off was not easy to come by at Clanville Lodge. Work, eat, sleep, was the daily routine. I loved the cows and the field work was much

Reg Smeeton, Farm Manager.

the same as at other farms and harvesting drew help from all round and about the village. Soldiers, the publican, the postman and other farmhands who could be spared helped during any farm harvesting. Tom Mathews came to the farm to help when off duty from his camp. At first Tom criticised the leisurely way we moved around the farm and thought we needed livening up. A few days of harvesting soon changed his tune, when he returned home feeling crippled after long hours of pitching corn. He was quite glad to get back to his airfield for a rest. He admitted he had no idea how hard farmers had to work. He had imagined they had a rather pleasant and easy life, and were overpaid for it.

Despite the company in the fields during that busy time, I was soon wondering what I had really gained by leaving Sparsholt. The Heath family spent quite a bit of their time in London, and I grew to look forward to the absence of the Captain. He could be very amiable and encouraging at times, and could be just as hard to please at others. He was not very fit, so was moody. Reg Smeeton, the farm manger, was always helpful and appreciative, so life was happier for me when he was in charge.

There were times when I was given the task of scrubbing down a cow each day to prepare her for a show and sale at Reading. On one occasion a well-known cattle photographer, named Hosegood, came to the farm to photograph some of the best cows. This took a whole morning. They were stood in longish grass, to show up their nice deep bodies. Their legs had to be placed to show off their good udders, their tails held down in their neat position and backs brushed down with water, to show how good and straight they were. It was quite a trying morning's work as the cows invariably moved just as the camera clicked. The Captain was unwell and in bed while this performance was going on and was disappointed to miss it but he was very pleased with the resultant photographs, which certainly did justice to his lovely animals and helped with their sale. What patience Mr Hosegood displayed.

When the Captain was unwell and not around the farm, Lady Marjorie would come round and inspect our work. She did her best to hustle me into doing everything at top speed and was very critical of all I was doing. One day she found the churns not clean enough, though I thought I had scrubbed them thoroughly. It was of course a serious matter to put milk into churns that were at all suspect, so I understood her concern but had never been given such a ferocious telling off in my life. The fact that she dragged me back to the farm, when I had been given a couple of hours off annoyed me too, but I had no sympathy from the Smeetons, who were shocked at my being careless with the churn washing, though I told them I had rarely done any washing up in my life as Mother preferred us out of her kitchen and had a woman to help her.

I sometimes was able to get to church on Sunday mornings, if we finished the milking in good time. The Vicar, the Reverend Northcott-Green, was very elderly and had a small congregation, so when I turned up he wanted to know who I was, and whether I was baptised and confirmed, and where and when. He took me to the Vicarage to show me a photo of his twelve children, and he had a signed photo of the Princess Royal, as his son was their tutor for a time. He told me he would come and see me at Clanville Lodge, and did not seem to approve of me working on the farm.

A few days later, the cow I was milking jumped in fright as a voice boomed out just behind her, "So here you are, under a cow!" It was indeed the Vicar keeping his promise to call on me. Miss Knight, across the shed, seeing me having a job to keep the bucket of milk safe from the startled animal, came across and said she would finish milking Primrose while I took the Vicar to Mrs Smeeton's who would be glad to give us tea. Sarah Smeeton rose to the occasion, though a little surprised to be entertaining the Vicar mid-afternoon, and quickly produced a pot of tea and a biscuit. Little three-year-old Cynthia was introduced and, hearing her sisters were at school, Mrs Smeeton was persuaded by the Vicar to let them join his children's choir. It was explained they would most likely only be able to attend when I was free to accompany them. I made excuse to be allowed to return to the milking and left Mrs Smeeton entertaining Mr Northcott-Green. I received a bit of ragging by Smeeton and Janie Knight about the visit – getting out of the milking and drinking afternoon tea instead.

The visit resulted in me accompanying not only Mary and Lucy Smeeton to church, but Thea and Myrna, Lois and Zella as well quite often. The

Reg & Sarah Smeeton and their three daughters: Mary, Lucy and Cynthia.

Smeetons sometimes came with the children, and were pleased to see the girls in the choir, quite enjoying the experience. I found I was often helped to get to a service on Sundays after that, with the children accompanying me. As it was never certain whether we could afford time off for half a day, I was glad of any respite. Generally one could count on a few hours off on Saturdays, between milkings, but I rarely got to shops. I often found I was carrying several weekly wage packets in my breeches pockets, before being able to bank them. It helped my savings nicely.

By October, I was seriously beginning to wonder whether a quiet life of routine farm work on a small farm, where my work was not really appreciated by my employer, was really the way I wanted to spend the rest of the war. The war news at the time was of the gallant prolonged fight the Russians were putting up in defence of Stalingrad and the dreadful suffering involved; there was no sign of a speedy return to normal peaceful life.

The Captain surprised me when he suddenly told me he thought I would be wise to look for better accommodation for the winter, as the cottage would be dismal in poor weather conditions. I heartily agreed, but was reluctant to tell Tom and Thea Mathews I wanted to move. They had been very hospitable.

To make things more difficult, after Tom had been on operations and away for some weeks and I had been company for Thea and had minded the children if she was out in the evening, Tom returned full of excitement to tell us he had been instructed to attend an interview at the War Office with Sir Archibald Sinclair. He had no idea why, but felt it was some sort of an honour as his Officer seemed to think this should be an excitement for him. When he returned he was very thrilled to have been thanked by Sir Archibald for the courageous and most helpful photography he had done after having been parachuted behind enemy lines in Europe. He was told he was to be promoted to officer rank, and was to report to an Officer Training Unit straightaway.

I felt it was not the moment to talk of leaving them, so waited until

Tom returned, full of tales of life at Camp. They had been instructed to always 'walk tall', heads held high, as they were the cream of the British defence. Tom clearly had gained tremendously in confidence and self-assurance. When the excitement had died down a bit, I did discuss with them the advantage for me of moving to live on the farm during the winter. To my joy, the Smeetons readily offered me a room in their home. I assured Thea I would always be prepared to spend the evening with the children when she was needed helping with social events at local camps. Though apparently quite sorry that Thea would not always have my company on dark winter evenings, they appreciated how much easier it would be for me to be on the farm, so we parted very amicably.

The Smeeton family made me so welcome; life was very enjoyable and I was thoroughly spoilt by Mrs Smeeton. Every morning, on going downstairs, a cup of tea awaited me and my gumboots were warmed and aired by the fire, and Mrs Smeeton was always cheerful, sending me out in good heart.

I was quite excited to be told by Smeeton that we were to go to a neighbouring farm to spread lime for Captain Prior-Palmer. The job was not pleasant, as it turned out, as we were shovelling lime from the back of a cart, in quite a brisk wind, and I inhaled a lot, despite having a head-scarf over my face. When I got in for tea, I had a severe nosebleed which took some time to ease off, so the next day was greeted with rather less excitement, though the weather was kinder. January to March was dogged by illness. The Captain was often ill and spent much time away; then the Smeeton children introduced us all to colds which they picked up at school. Mr and Mrs Smeeton had to retire to bed with severe colds or 'flu, and Reg Smeeton developed a pneumonic lung so was off work for some weeks, keeping Janie Knight and me very busy. It was all pretty depressing.

I was relieved to hear Alan had landed safely in North Africa, after their boat had been sunk in the Mediterranean.

We had all made great efforts to send Alan on his way with plenty of cigarettes by scouring the area for likely sources of supply; also films for his camera, razor blades, a supply of family photos and even sweets. It was sad to think of him landing, with no possessions, dressed only in a blanket. He had little time to be concerned, as he was into a fierce gun battle almost at once. We heard later that he had severe damage to a leg and would have had an amputation but for the recent discovery of penicillin. He was transferred from the artillery to an intelligence unit.

In March the good news came that Enid had given birth to Bill's son, to be named Stewart. Bill, by now in Basutoland at a training camp for African recruits, was to wait four long years before meeting his son.

When the Heaths returned to the farm the Captain was still very unwell, and it was pretty well impossible for me to do anything that pleased him. Receiving an occasional card from a friend, Patrick Davy, who spent most of the war in a German prisoner camp, made me feel ashamed to complain about my occupation. I did however decide to change my job, though I would miss the Smeetons a lot.

At Easter – at the end of April – the war news that the Allies were winning the battle in Tunisia, and that Rommel had been moved to another area and was likely to meet with defeat in North Africa, brought us some cheer and hope that the end of the war might be in sight. Germany was suffering a great bombardment from the air also. It did not lift my spirits greatly, but I was job hunting, and applying for jobs I saw advertised in the *Farmers' Weekly*. I should have asked the WLA about a transfer, but was keen not to fall for another job like the present one. How often I had wished I had asked advice from Mr Ashenden before leaving Sparsholt.

I met Joy Gane sometimes, and Gwen Hunt, and we laughed together over our happy days at the Institute. I was pleased to be told, when Tutt the vet attended both Sparsholt and Clanville Lodge, that Jack had told him he had never had as good a worker helping him since I left. I was asked by Mr Tutt if I would go and work for his mother. I was not keen on the idea of working for a woman, so declined, with thanks.

I received offers of work in reply to my applications, but was not drawn to any until I read of applications required for the job of Forewoman for Land Girls working for Wiltshire War Agricultural Committee. It sounded to be just the sort of work to give me a complete change and, perhaps, my Sparsholt experience of training girls would be of value. I sent an application, hoping the WLA would allow me to change counties if my application was successful. I received a reply, asking me to obtain permission to change counties before my application could be given consideration. It was not too easy getting that permission but, after going to Winchester, and being reproached for not applying to my County HQ for a change of farm, my pleas prevailed, and I was able to confirm that I was allowed to move to Wiltshire, should I be appointed to the job.

I received at last the letter I hoped for, inviting me to Trowbridge to be interviewed for the Forewoman post on 25th May. The following week I received a letter from the Wilts War Ag. Labour Officer, Michael Culham, offering me the job to start on 7th June. I had written a note to the Captain, before the interview in Wiltshire, giving him my notice, so the short notice I received from Mr Culham about starting work was no problem. I was unable to take leave of the Captain as he was confined to bed, very ill.

Janie Knight had always been pretty kindly and uncritical to work with and she seemed genuinely sorry when I gave in my notice. I saw very little of Lady Marjorie, and she ignored me when we passed on the farm, though whether she was aggravated that I should leave while the Captain was ill and unavailable, or whether she was preoccupied with worry I could not assess, since the family were apt to ignore staff quite often if concerned with other affairs. Janie did tell me, however, that Lady Marjorie would double my wages if I would agree to stay on, as she did not want the Captain worried. I told Janie that I would not be working at weekends at my Wilts job,

COUNTY OF WILTS

WAR AGRICULTURAL EXECUTIVE COMMITTEE

Telephone No. : 711 (3 lines).
Telegraphic Address :
  " Husbandry, Trowbridge."
Communications should be
addressed to the
  EXECUTIVE OFFICER
Postage MUST be prepaid

AGRICULTURAL DEPT.

COUNTY HALL,

TROWBRIDGE,

WILTS.

Our Ref. MGC/JFC   2nd June, 1943.

Your Ref. _____

Miss A. Hall,
c/o Mrs. Smeeton,
Clanville Lodge Farm,
Andover.

Dear Miss Hall,

Thank you for your letter of the
26th May. I am very glad to know you
will be able to commence duties on the
7th instant with this Committee. I
should be glad if you would report to
the "George & Dragon" Potterne, Near
Devizes to see Miss G. Steer the Committee's
forewoman at this hostel. I will ask her
to arrange for you to have a billet, and
make the other necessary arrangements.

I would also inform that your
wage will be £3 per week plus overtime
at the standard agricultural rate. Whilst
at Potterne you will be under the
direction of Mr. N.E. Brown.

Yours truly,

M.G. CULHAM
Labour Officer.

and would start in Salisbury, while learning the work, so could help them at weekends voluntarily until they found a replacement. Janie told me I would be welcome if I was able to do so until the harvest was in.

Leaving the Smeetons was easier, knowing that I could return sometimes for weekends, but I felt no great elation at departing as I travelled home tediously slowly on stopping trains, and having several waits at changes. I was aware of feeling very drained. Seeing my father waiting with the car quickly lightened my mood, with the thought of a whole new start ahead.

10 Wiltshire WAEC Trainee Forewoman

June 1943

SUNDAY 6TH JUNE BEING MY one day between jobs, was one of frantic activity – sorting, washing and pressing such clothes as would be needed for the role of forewoman in charge of a gang. Hopefully no more smelly, dung-splashed dungarees, but tidy breeches with jacket or overall.

I was persuaded by my sister Jill to accompany her for a look round Bournemouth as a brief respite. It was sad to see J.E. Beales, our favourite store, now just a heap of rubble, since on May 23rd, 1943, a number of German aircraft avoided radar detection by flying in at sea level to drop four tons of explosives on the centre of Bournemouth. Woolworths and Bobbys were destroyed but the greatest tragedy was the bombing of two large hotels and a hundred Canadian Servicemen died in the direct hit on the Metropole Hotel at Lansdown. It was a week before all the bodies could be recovered. Such a tragic waste of young life sent one back to work with a fresh zeal to see this wretched war through to victory and peace.

Mother came for the bus ride to Salisbury on Monday and saw me off to Devizes by bus – a cheering start to what turned out to be a tiresome day, and not the welcome I had hoped to receive. Though told to report to Potterne, no one there was expecting me. The forewoman consulted Mr Brown, the assistant Labour Officer. He told me to stay the night and he would look in at Potterne Hostel tomorrow and, in the meantime, consult with Mr Culham to find out where I should go.

After a somewhat sleepless night in a noisy hostel and an uncomfortable, narrow, hard bed, I was thankful to greet Mr Brown and to be taken back to Salisbury to comfortable and welcoming digs in Harnham – a lovely house with an attractive garden running down to the river. Mrs Brewer made me most welcome, and the twelve days I was with her were wonderful. If I had been her daughter she could not have done more to make me comfortable and feel very much at home.

I was to have a training time with Miss Hay, the Forewoman of the Salisbury WLA gang. I was to meet her lorry on the nearby main road, at the petrol pumps of a big garage, at 7.30 the next day. I was awoken by Mrs Brewer with a large bun and a cup of tea at 6.15, and after a large cooked breakfast she insisted on accompanying me to the garage, as she felt it unsafe to be out alone so early in the morning. Miss Hay had an authoritative, quite brisk manner but, once in the front seat of the lorry with her, she gave me helpful information and advice about the role of Forewomen. The work today was to be potato hoeing.

In Winterbourne Stoke we were turned out into a large field armed with our hoes, and I worked alongside the gang leader, Aino Trumees, whose home was Estonia. We made good progress with the hoeing as I listened to Aino's tales of life as a Russian citizen, but the lunch break was welcome after four hours of hoeing with just a ten minute rest at mid-morning to have coffee from our flasks. By 3 o'clock not only was my back groaning, but blisters were threatening on my hands. It seemed to me a much longer day than when working on different jobs on a general farm. At 5.30 came the 'knock-off' whistle from Miss Hay, who was in the lorry writing up time sheets. While cleaning my hoe and climbing back into the lorry cab, I was telling myself I would soon be able to organise my time supervising a gang instead of being a gang member, but this was valuable in learning what it was like for girls in the gang.

On returning to my digs, Mrs Brewer was concerned at our long day of work and insisted on punting me down the river to let me relax completely. It was novel indeed for a Land Girl to be so treated, and I was most grateful. I was with Mrs Brewer for my first nine days of gang work, and it was her kindness and concern that kept me going. Working day after day as a gang member was not the work I had expected but while I was so employed, Miss Hay was not needed and found occupation elsewhere. The warm welcome home, the good food and company each day and the relaxing punting down the river in the cool of the evening were very reviving.

Mr Culham told me to return home and take driving lessons for a week. This was a welcome break and proved enjoyable with roads quite clear on account of severe petrol rationing. With morning lessons only it proved something of a holiday and I returned in good heart to the gang work. I was moved to new digs as my place at Mrs Brewer's was now filled. At Mrs Allen's, another kindly home, though not as luxurious, I was well fed and looked after. On the walls of my little bedroom were unusual pictures, including one of a little girl sitting on her mother's tombstone, over the text: 'Thy will be done'. On the other wall a text – 'Be strong and of good courage'. Whilst I could not believe God wills that little girls should mourn over their dead mother's grave, I felt perhaps I needed the advice given in the other!

By the end of June I must have achieved miles of hoeing; I had worked hard on threshing many a very dirty rick of beans, or corn, pulled acres of flax, repaired cornfields on the plains damaged by army tanks taking the wrong routes. I was becoming more and more convinced that I was in the wrong job as this was not the Forewoman work I had applied for. Seeing Mr Brown coming towards me across the field, I was about to tell him how I felt when, to my relief, he told me that Mr Culham wanted me to go at once to digs in Trowbridge, as I was to start lorry driving instruction. Mr Culham had become impatient with the time Miss Hay was keeping me for 'instruction'. I was soon settled in excellent digs in Trowbridge at 78, Whiterow Park with Mrs Gleed, widow of a farmer. It was a happy billet with someone who knew all about land work.

Reporting to Mr Butler of Fore Street Garage the next morning, I found myself in the driving seat of an ex-Naval five-ton Austin lorry, with green canvas cover. I found the long side mirrors saw little beyond that billowing canvas. When reversing I had to lean some distance out to look round it. With my short legs I had a job to keep in the long travel of the clutch to reverse slowly. I did however feel more confident driving forward in the lorry than in my father's little Triumph Scorpion car. It was an advantage in narrow lanes to be able to see over the hedges from the high lorry cab. The lorry had a very poor lock so I was glad of the expert tuition I gained about how to use the steering to best advantage, especially in reversing. After ten days I was despatched on my first solo drive to go to Mere Hostel to take charge of a gang of twenty girls.

Aino, trainee lorry driver, with 'my' lorry, Jane.

Despite being very nervous, all went well on the drive until I approached Mere and realized I was about to descend the steep winding hill I had been warned about. Mr Butler told me I must change to a low gear before starting down this hill. Having stopped, a coach suddenly passed me with the driver raving very impolite remarks in my direction and the passengers gesticulating angrily. Obviously I had all but caused a disastrous collision. I was still pretty shaky on finding the hostel down a narrow lane. Mr Brown told me I would have to pass the hostel to reverse the lorry through the gate. This I managed, but only to find I had taken the far post in with me. By this time the Land Girls had emerged and found it very funny. Fortunately, Mr Brown was very cheerful about it and congratulated me on having achieved something other drivers had tried to do, and was happy I had made the entrance much easier for them in future.

Mr Brown told me that Mr Culham would be looking in some evening to see if there were any difficulties, but he thought I would find Mere Gang friendly and good workers, so there should not be any problems. I was pleased that Mr Culham was coming as I had met him several times while in Trowbridge and found him very easy to talk to.

Having been shown my room, May, the gang leader, escorted me to meet the warden and I had my meal with her. I was relieved to be told that Reg (a conchie) was taking Italian prisoners to work on the same farm as Mere Gang, in the morning, so I would have a pilot. We were likely to be working for Mr Jeffrey at Donhead St. Mary for some time on a flax pulling job. With all road signs removed for the duration of the war, good map reading was essential, though helped by Labour Officers giving instructions by phone most evenings.

Flax pulling was hard on the hands and tiring so I was pleased to find willing workers and I was able to spend some time walking round and working with different groups to get to know as many of the girls as possible, trying to memorise names and find out what sort of work they had done pre-war. They were friendly and I felt I knew some fairly well by the end of the day.

11 WWAEC: Mere Gang

July - August 1943

MY FIRST SUNDAY WAS RESTFUL and enjoyable. I was pleased to have eleven of the girls accompanying me to the village church for Matins, and they were a friendly lot. The rest of the day I was on my own – I got down to catching up on correspondence, and spent time with Mrs Andrews, getting to know her. Some of the girls asked me if I would like to go with them to an evening E.N.S.A. concert, but I declined with thanks. They would have enough of me at work, without having me around in the evenings.

As it turned out I had made the right decision as the next morning to my surprise the gang suddenly refused to go to work until there was some improvement in hostel food and their daily packed lunch. I had a shrewd suspicion this was, in part, a testing of my authority. I simply reminded them that they would of course lose their day's pay if they did not work, and I would talk to Lady McNeil about their complaint and see how matters could be improved. With reluctance they slowly climbed up into the lorry, muttering about not being able to do much work if not properly fed. Once in the field I realized I was having to deal with a 'go slow'. I spent the day chasing up the girls, and got more tired walking round and round the field keeping them hard at it than if I had given a hand with the work. I wrote down the names of the worst of the slackers, and this had an effect on the rest of the gang whose effort improved so that a good day's work was achieved. On returning to the hostel, an invitation to an Army dance that evening soon raised morale.

Cheered by an enjoyable evening in the company of the soldiers, the rest of the week went well with no more slacking and no more strike talk. I was promised by Lady McNeil that the WLA Pioneer

Warden, Mrs Anderson, would be coming to the hostel to assess the situation as soon as she was free of her present similar assignment elsewhere.

With girls coming to me for travel warrants and requests for the loan of rail fares, I was reminded the weekend was August Bank Holiday. I felt ready for a break, as it was a bit of a strain keeping a right relationship with the girls and yet ensuring that the farmers were satisfied they were getting a good day's work from the gang. My gang leader was a good worker and very helpful in keeping the girls working when I was called away to transport school children, conchies or prisoners-of-war to other harvest work, as the War Ag. used any labour available. I was glad of the experience it gave me with the lorry and felt my reversing, turning and coping with narrow lanes was improving.

Mr Culham kept in touch and seemed to think I was a pretty strict Forewoman. He asked me to prepare for him a report on each of the members of the gang, as he and Lady McNeil and Mr McClure the Labour Officer would be paying the gang an official visit soon. He then told me I would not be staying with Mere gang for very long as he wanted me to tackle a larger and troublesome gang in the north of the County. I did not really want to think yet about a move, having just begun to settle in Mere and to feel at home with this gang but made no comment, other than agreeing to let him have the report on the Mere girls. I think he was quite impressed to be told Mere gang, during the past week, had cleared forty-five acres of flax and were well into the next thirty-six acres, and Mr Jeffrey was well satisfied with their efforts.

After Mr Culham had left, Mr McClure looked in to see how things were going, and I said I felt quite sad I was only to have a short stay in Mere. Then he left, leaving me pondering his last remark: "I think it wise to have an early move on this job, as one always makes mistakes when one is new to a job, and it gives one a fresh start to benefit by the mistakes." As I journeyed home I had plenty of time to think of all the mistakes I might benefit from. It was good to find family at the station and forget Wilts War Ag. for a couple of days.

There was a cheerful air about the hostel as we all returned refreshed from a restful weekend of home comforts. There were still grumbles about the food, but even so I was pleased that the girls readily agreed to a request from Mr Jeffrey that the gang might work late all week as his men were to work till 8.30 pm to press on with the corn harvest. Unfortunately the weather did not co-operate and we battled to get stooks to stand against strong winds and heavy showers, which meant much turning of the stooks each day to try to get them to dry out.

Mr. McClure with Aino Trumees (right) and the author (left).

Though the complaints about Mrs Andrews and her running of the hostel increased, considering the tiring work and very long hours I was pleased at the way the girls kept going. It was very cheering to us all that Mrs Anderson, the very kindly pioneer warden, should turn up at this time. How the food and the general comfort of the hostel at once improved. Mrs Andrews was very upset at this turn of events and resigned and left. Mrs Anderson carried on until a new and more acceptable staff was appointed. I very much enjoyed Mrs

Anderson's company, and spent time with her each evening, instead of being on my own in my room.

When told the gang was to move to another farm for the next week and resume normal hours we were relieved, but I was sad to learn I was to lose May. May was needed in Salisbury gang while Aino came to help me, and to fit in some lorry driving practice. Though Aino was one to keep the gang working well, the gang knew her and were delighted to hear she was to join Mere gang. The gang were not so happy to hear the next farm we were going to was Mr Caddy's. The girls said he was a slavedriver, and would swear at the girls if he thought they were not giving their best all day. I was not too surprised, therefore, to receive a lecture from him on our arrival, telling me how I was to do my job. I just listened, and was amused when he later came to say we were doing a good hoeing job, but then he wanted us to go to the wheat field. We were to walk ahead of the cutter and binder to pull out wild vetches. Though we must have walked miles it was not arduous and at least made a change. We were then invited to eat our packed lunches in Stourton Vicarage. We were treated to hot drinks, and the Vicar's wife produced her camera to snap us picnicking. We all appreciated eating indoors, for a change, and not under a hedge. I left the gang in Aino's charge in the afternoon and visited some of the gang at Mr White's farm and waited to collect them.

Life in the hostel was now happier for the girls, as it was for me, having Mrs Anderson's company for evening walks and companionship. 'Andy' had helped the girls to form their own entertainment committee to plan evening activity, sometimes in the hostel, but quite often going to local dances, or films, or the occasional ENSA show. They were encouraged to entertain their soldier friends in the hostel also. One weekend, the girls came and asked if I would be allowed to use the lorry on a Sunday as, having done so much harvesting, they would like to attend an open-air Harvest Thanksgiving they had read about on a local poster. It was to be led by the Bishop of Salisbury at a farm at Kingston Deverill. I was readily given permission by

Mr Culham, as he was to be at the service and would be glad to have Land Girls represented, since they did help tremendously in harvesting. I was proud of my smart girls in uniform and almost dazzled by the very well-polished shoes all along the benches in the lorry when I went round to fasten up the tailboard.

We assembled around neat ricks of newly harvested corn and hay ricks in a corner of a large field. We had just sung 'Come Ye Thankful People Come' and the Bishop was leading in prayer when thunder rumbled overhead and, almost simultaneously, the rain lashed down and we had no option but to rush back to cars and back into the lorry, looking damp and dishevelled, with the girls' well-polished shoes all mud-splashed. Their disappointment at having to return to the hostel turned to excitement when they realized Mr Culham was following the lorry to the hostel, and was accompanied by the Bishop. After the service was taken in the hostel, tea was served to Mr Culham and

Eleven of Mere Gang having lunched at Sturton Vicarage while on a nearby hoeing job for Mr. Caddy. Back row: Nancy Arnold, Kathleen Clear, Marie Noke, Terry Merriman, Hilda Browning, Amy Mitchell. Front row: Eileen Leaving, Margaret Gouldman, Vicky Norris, Mavis Hussey, Sylvia Bolland.

the Bishop; the girls were invited to join this rather special tea when the Bishop chatted to us all. To round off this excitement twenty-seven servicemen turned up in the evening in response to the entertainment committee's invitation to spend an evening with the girls. Further light refreshments were served, so it proved to be a very happy day after all. No more grumbles were heard about hostel life.

The following week's work was a bit of an anti-climax: a very heavy, hard-going, hoeing of turnips, in a sea of thick mud. The farmer was in no good humour, but the girls bore it all well. The week ended with Mr Culham, Lady McNeil and Mr McClure coming to see the girls, individually, to discuss with them my report. The only unhappy outcome was the dismissing of a girl from the WLA by Lady McNeil for being a disgrace to the WLA, having behaved badly and been brought home very drunk from an army dance. Though she was not a good worker, we all felt sorry for her leaving in that way.

All too soon came the end of my time with Mere gang. Mr Culham's warning that the Corsham gang to which he was now sending me was a much tougher proposition, which had proved too much for other forewomen, did nothing to make me happier about leaving Mere, where things were running very smoothly. On my last Sunday all the girls decided to accompany me to Matins, and all dressed smartly in uniform. I said goodbye to the vicar at 8am service; he did look a little surprised at this parade and perhaps, like me, wondered if the fact that it was a soldiers' parade service had in any way influenced the good Land Army attendance.

The next day proved an ordeal of sad farewells as I waved the gang off to work and stacked my luggage into the van sent to collect me for Corsham. We called in at County Hall and Mr Culham assured me I would have excellent support from Mr Keevil, my Labour Officer in Chippenham and, if I was faced with difficulties, that I should not hesitate to contact him at County Hall. I said I hoped I could rise to the challenge and would keep him in touch with progress.

12 Lypiatt Hostel – Corsham Gang
August 1943 - January 1944

ROSEMARY HEADLEY, THE FOREWOMAN I was to replace with the Corsham gang, gave me a warm welcome. She was thankful I was to relieve her of responsibility for a gang with a poor work reputation. The tiresome gang and grumbling farmers had many times reduced Rosemary to tears. All in all, Corsham did not strike me as a very welcome prospect after the happy Mere gang.

Rosemary took me along to her room, which I was to share until she left. It was typical hostel style – two camp-style beds with lumpy mattresses, two small wardrobes and two small chests and upright chairs for each of us. Having shed my luggage I was taken across an open grass area to the main building which had a reception hall, a recreation hall, a dining canteen, and a pleasant buffet, where we were served with coffee and delicious cheese and onion sandwiches. The single-storey huts surrounding this building, such as 'P' and 'Q' blocks, which were our Land Army accommodation, were mostly occupied by Irish workers employed at a nearby underground aircraft factory. These workers, being on shift work, were no company for the Land Girls, but they found friends in the adjoining Royal Marines' camp. Rosemary told me I had to see that the Marines were not entertained in the WLA huts but only in the buffet, or the entertainment hall, where there were frequent films, ENSA or CEEMA shows, and dances.

September 1st was a pouring wet day so the girls were 'rained off'. This was a chance to meet some of my gang, and I was introduced to Miss Bartram and Miss Fernee, my Gang Leaders. Both were in their thirties and full of self-confidence. They had worked together in a Carreras cigarette factory in London pre-war. Their attitude was somewhat cool, but they introduced me to the WLA Hostel Warden, Miss Hobday. She was a dear, and loved her Land Girls. A keen Baptist Christian, she invited me to attend the weekly 'Padre's Hour' run by a Baptist Minister in a small chapel in the main building, and I readily accepted. She was amused to hear I was only twenty-three-years-old as the girls had told her I was about forty. (I had long hair dragged back into a rather severe-looking bun.) I hoped they would continue to think me old as it might help me in asserting my authority. Miss Hobday took me into her room and told me to drop in whenever I liked, if in need of help or just a chat. I was told there was a sick-bay almost opposite our blocks with an excellent nursing sister in charge, should I be anxious about the health of any of the gang. I was heartened to have this good friend in 'Q' Block, and looked forward to meeting others at the Padre's Hour.

I was unhappy with Rosemary's lorry, aptly named 'Who'd 'a' thought it'. It was a large Fordson, and not only was the travel on the clutch too much for my short legs, making me feel unsafe driving it, but the gear lever, behind my left arm, at waist height, I found very awkward to manage. As rain made it impossible to work and Rosemary wanted to go to Trowbridge to see Mr Culham, I decided that would allow me to visit the lorry depot and ask Mr Bowley for another Austin lorry such as I was used to. I was greatly relieved to be given a new Austin, sister model to 'Emma', my Mere lorry. 'Jane' was now to serve me well for a long time, and I felt greater confidence in driving my new gang.

Mr Culham seemed pleased to see us and said Rosemary could stay with me for another week before moving to Salisbury. He told me he had just been reading unfavourable reports from farmers about the unsatisfactory work of the Corsham gang. I was told any action I felt necessary to get the gang working would get his backing. He intended to have a meeting in a week's time, to hear my report on the girls. Mr Keevil, Mrs Methuen, our local Rep., and Lady Catherine McNeil, WLA County Organiser, would meet him at Corsham to take any necessary action, on hearing my report and recommendations.

On our return to Corsham, cheered by the outing, we enjoyed the popular cheese and onion sandwiches in the snack bar whilst waiting for Mr Keevil to phone directions to Bowden Hill Farm, where we were to work the next day. Mr Keevil asked us to leave Bart and Fernee supervising the potato picking at the farm as he would like us to see him at the Chippenham office. This suited our plan to get Humphries Garage in Chippenham to make a foot hole in the new lorry tailboard, as the girls experienced difficulty in getting up into the lorry without this help. After a friendly chat with Mr Keevil about working with the Corsham gang, it was not quite time to collect the lorry, so Rosemary and I lunched in Phelps, the nice little Chippenham cafe – a pleasant change from the usual field picnic on a dry sandwich. I was back with the gang by 2.30 and thinking about the report expected of me in a week's time; I spent the rest of the afternoon watching the girls at work and making notes as I went round getting to know names.

That evening Rosemary and I attended a service in the hostel chapel, as it was a special 'Day of Prayer' to mark the fourth anniversary of the outbreak of war. During the service, we heard with joy of the successful invasion of Italy by the British forces, which meant the breaking of the Axis with Germany. We all gave thanks, hoping this could be the beginning of the end of this devastating conflict.

On leaving the assembly hall Rosemary introduced me to Mr Yarnold, the Hostel Manager, who came to tell me I was wanted on the phone. It was Culham – he felt very happy about the news, but did not have anything specific to say about work, except that he felt sure I was going to be a success and that I would be happy in Corsham. How I wished I could share his confidence. It was going to be a lonely role once Rosemary had left. It was not going to be easy to get to know all these girls who already seemed to suspect I was there to make them work harder. I was aware of a hostile attitude in some already.

Saturday afternoon provided us with a pleasant break. Rosemary and I took a train to Bath. It was bliss to get away from the noisy hostel to this beautiful city. We browsed around the abbey, and then around the shops. When passing a hairdressers, on the spur of the moment I decided to get rid of my bun. In next to no time I came out feeling a new person with a neat short bob. After a nice cafe tea we returned to Corsham in very light-hearted mood. From then on I was known as 'Bob' to the other Forewomen, until later they changed the nickname to 'Cock Robin'. Did they, I wonder, think of me then as Cocky Robin, but stopped short of saying so? I decided to watch my step.

The next week was not very happy for any of us. On Monday it was decided to try out the new Forewoman, and some took too long over breakfast and dawdled along to the lorry. Some were still missing, ignoring my warning, at 7.40 am, so I closed up the tailboard and, despite the cries of protest, I drove off without the latecomers. This meant they would lose a day's pay – there was fury in the camp. The next day none came to the lorry until 8 am, knowing I could not drive off without any girls. I said nothing and there was much giggling among the gang. At 5 pm some were setting off to the lorry but I made them return to do the half hour's work they still owed because of the late start. The farm agent agreed they must work the time for which they were paid. After getting back late for supper, missing their dates, and getting no sympathy from anyone, there was no further trouble about leaving the hostel on time.

Though there were troublemakers and slackers in the gang, many of the girls were co-operative and good workers. After tackling the gang leaders for tolerating the slackers and rebels and warning them I might need new gang leaders, I got full co-operation from them and we became friends. They began to appreciate the discipline and knew I was busy writing up my report to give to the Committee on Friday.

The work at Bowden Hill Estate was not a happy experience because Mr Croft, the agent, had a poor opinion of the Corsham gang and, though the girls worked satisfactorily in difficult conditions, they could not do anything right for him. He tried to tell me how to do my job, so our relationship was distant and his advice ignored.

Rosemary, however, was really enjoying working with Corsham gang now she had shed the responsibility for discipline. She was quite sad when the time came for her to leave, and I knew I was going to miss her a lot. I was not able to socialise with the girls after work; they had quite enough of me on the job. When the fateful Friday came Rosemary left early, and I had to prepare to meet the little committee. Having been introduced by Mr Culham, I gave to each committee member my written report on each of the girls. The girls were then called in, in turn. Several slackers were offered a move to other gangs and some preferred to leave the WLA. Troublemakers were split up and sent to different gangs elsewhere. All were given a reminder about the great importance of their work on food production in wartime. The good co-operators were praised on getting good reports and encouraged to work for a good work reputation for the gang. Before leaving, Mr Culham had a chat with me in his car and seemed pleased with the way the evening went. As he drove off I felt very alone making my way in the dark to the snack bar.

With the moving of some of the gang, the dismissal of others and some new intake coming to replace them, some of the girls were moody and quarrelsome. I would have to find a way to change the mood when they got over this upset. While harvesting acre after acre of potatoes, the girls were tired and there was quarrelling as to who was being set to gather up the longest rows. The agreeable farmers for whom we were working were upset by all this bad temper as they were pleased with the girls' work.

On the way home, stopping for petrol, I went round to the back of the lorry and told the gang I could appreciate how tired they were, but the farmers had been appreciative and considerate and had spoken of sending in a very favourable report on their work to the War Ag. It would be nice if they showed them what cheerful workers they could be as I had been asked if it would be in order to give the girls a 'tip'. Maybe they could cheer us and passersby with a sing-song on the way home. As we set off again I was delighted to catch strains of 'Give me land lots of land, and a starry sky above, don't fence me in'. Back at the hostel, as they stumbled stiffly from the lorry, I was met with a few smiles, which gave me much needed cheer and encouragement.

At Lower Stanton, working for Mr Jones, a former submarine commander, the girls were thanked for their hard work and given five shillings tip each as they left. This was exactly the encouragement they needed and deserved and it transformed their attitude to work. Back to Bowden Farm Mr Croft was as difficult to please, so I put in a complaint to the War Ag. about the way he tried to interfere with my management of the gang and his general attitude to our work. We were moved on to Mr Cuff's farm at Langley Burrell. Despite a bitterly cold morning the girls ran around chasing each other to get warm until the potato spinner arrived and work started. Mr Cuff and his tractor driver were amazed at the girls' speed and thoroughness. Mr Cuff told me he was very annoyed that when he rang the War Ag. to tell them how satisfied he was with the Land Girls they all laughed and thought he was being sarcastic. Mr Keevil came to see for himself how the work was going and, though pleased with Corsham gang, was not pleased to have been asked for Hullavington gang also, only to find they had been sent back to their hostel. Mr Keevil was clearly astonished when I told him the Gang would like to attend Corsham Church on Sunday, and he told me I might take the lorry for this outing.

St. Bartholomew Church, Corsham, is set in the grounds of Corsham Court, home of the Methuen family. Mrs Methuen, as our local Rep., visited the girls every week for a chat, to sort out problems or order any new uniform needed. The girls loved her, so seeing her surprise and delight when she came into church added to their enjoyment, as most of the girls were not churchgoers and a little unsure of how they would be received. The service was a Harvest Thanksgiving Matins and Communion. I was pleased Margaret Thompson joined me at the Communion rail, the only one who was confirmed. The Army parade the same day meant there was a pleasant bit of fraternising after service, before getting into the lorry. Mrs Methuen told

Corsham W.L.A.: 'The Wonder Gang'. Forewoman 'Fernee' in front on the left.

me she was very proud of the smart turnout of her girls and hoped they would come again, which they often did after that.

After tea in the Canteen, as I crossed the green back to 'Q' Block, the church bells were playing the hymn tune, 'We love Thy church O God', and I found myself making my way to Evensong – a great service accompanied by an army band; we 'Ploughed the Fields and Scattered' almost to swing time. To drop into the familiar age-old canticles, psalms and hymns was a real 'Homecoming' – and a great spiritual uplift and a helpful start to another week.

At the end of September, working for Mr Brunt at Grittleton on a heavy crop of potatoes in a six-acre field, the girls worked well and kept at the job until 6.30 pm in order to finish the field. Mr Brunt was pleasant to work for and very appreciative. He had lovely horses; he bred Percherons, having a very handsome stallion, as well as lovely pure-bred Shires. He was interested that my paternal grandfather of Lancashire had bred Shires. I must have inherited my great love of these gentle giants from him, and I loved leading these handsome creatures.

Mr Brunt attended a meeting of the War Ag. Committee while we were working for him and said how pleased he was with the excellent work of the Corsham girls. To his annoyance, this was treated with disbelief, so he got Mr Culham to return to the field to see for himself the work the girls were doing. I had just returned to the lorry to do the time sheets as they arrived, so came in for a ragging about taking life easy while the gang worked. In fact the girls seemed to work better when I was able to watch them, which I could not easily do when working with them. Mr Culham was impressed that they were willingly putting in long hours on a heavy job. I told him I was going to ask the catering manager for a better lunch pack while doing extra hours, and he approved this.

The next day we were faced with just two acres of a light crop of potatoes and the work was finished by noon. Before we moved on to the neighbouring farm of Mr Harding, Mr Brunt gave two shillings and sixpence to each of the girls, and five shillings each to

Bart and Fernee. This caused much delight amongst the gang but when faced with great long rows of potatoes in a very large field at Mr Harding's, the excitement soon died down. The girls settled down under a hedge to eat their sandwiches in subdued silence while waiting for the arrival of the potato spinner. Once started they kept their backs bent, and cleared two acres of the field before the 'knock-off' whistle at 6.30. They did not proceed to a barn, as directed by Mr Harding, with much enthusiasm, but their reluctance turned to great joy when they found they were not faced by yet another little job of stacking potato sacks, or some such afterthought, but by a real peace-time feast arranged on a large table. Three loaves of bread, one pound of margarine, two pots of jam, two pounds of sugar, and three great jugs of tea. Mr and Mrs Harding enjoyed the girls' excitement and great appreciation.

There was no reluctance the next day to complete the job by 5pm. Mr Harding added to his kindness by getting Mr Keevil to give the girls the whole of the next day, Saturday, as a rest day, having heard the gang was to work on Sunday for Mr Maundrell. Working for Mr Maundrell was no problem. He was very satisfied with the way the gang harvested his potato crop. Praise then followed the gang's hard work at many farms, pulling mangolds in very cold weather. I was proud of the way they worked without any grumbling, despite the hard work and uncomfortable conditions.

Trainee forewomen were now turning up at Corsham to learn the Forewoman's role. Vera Long had joined me from Salisbury, and a new recruit for this work, Phyl Munro, needed to be introduced to the job, though she was a competent driver and farmworker. Phyl was a good disciplinarian, and my favourable report to Culham on her competence, led him to suggest Phyl should take over the Corsham gang, and I could move to Enford. I was enjoying Corsham, and had got used to the camp site and found other forewomen would often join me for a chat in the snack bar in the evenings.

I was relieved when Culham changed his mind and sent Phyl to run Enford gang instead of me. Mr Yarnold and Mr Edgely, the

Catering Manager, said they were pleased I did not have to leave, which was encouraging. They would sometimes join me in the assembly hall to watch the concerts, plays or films. The films were often silent, and we got great entertainment from the mainly Irish audience who would, very amusingly, provide the sound effects. Wolf whistles for heroines, boos for villains, and cheers for heroes. It added to what could have been dull entertainment.

In October I had to drive volunteer holidaying adults and sometimes older schoolchildren to help on farms with potato picking, and Italian prisoners from Chippenham POW camp also. Some of these young Italians had been prisoners a long time, and it was sad to hear from some that close relatives had died in their absence, or that their wives had left them. Their hope of being allowed home now that Italy had surrendered had not been realised and they were very disheartened. I felt sorry for them and for our boys in a similar situation. While I did this Fernee was mostly driving Corsham gang as I had another trainee forewoman doing lorry driving practice. Aleen had suffered the dreadful loss of her first babe with Pink's disease while her husband was serving abroad. By joining the War Ag. she hoped to help the war effort and recover somewhat from her tragic experience which she accepted very courageously. We became good friends and it was cheering to hear after the war that she and her husband had the joy of more children.

At the end of October I paid a final weekend visit to Clanville Lodge Farm as the Smeetons were leaving. I walked around the fields and said farewell to the beautiful Shorthorn cows with regret. I missed being with animals while doing so much field work. When the Captain died and the cattle were sold I read in the *Farmers' Weekly* that they made record prices for such pedigree cattle which pleased me, as they must have gone to good homes.

In December we were delighted to hear that the Duke of Beaufort's agent had made a request for Corsham gang to harvest a late potato crop on the estate. This involved getting special permission for a Wilts lorry to cross over the border into Gloucestershire. Having a WVS canteen coming daily to bring us lunch to the field was an unheard of luxury we greatly enjoyed. Another excitement was meeting Queen Mary very informally when she paid a visit to help saw up wood 'to keep the home fires burning'. The Queen Mother asked us from which hostel we came and was concerned to know if conditions were comfortable – there were a lot of letters written home that evening. A less happy meeting for me was when a gentleman complained that a tractor had driven over sacks of potatoes and my girls should move them. Having told him to tackle his tractor driver, not my girls, Fernee came up to ask what the Duke had been talking about. My face was a little red.

Just before taking four days' leave Michael Culham turned up on one of his evening visits and invited me into his car for a business talk, the gist of it being that Phyl Munro and I were to be promoted to assistants to our Labour Officers. Phyl was to be responsible for supervising the gangs, hostels, and forewomen in the south of the County and I was to take charge of the North. We would do a lot of touring on motorbikes to be readily available where needed. This promotion would earn us a rise in salary. Corsham would be mainly run by Fernee and Bart.

This gave me plenty to think about on the tedious train journey home with long waits at Corsham, Bath, Salisbury and Southampton. Having set off at 7.30 am, I arrived home at half-past four. My frustration quickly evaporated back with the family; Cara arrived just after me on a 48-hour leave from Portland, where she was then stationed in the WAAF. Though this break was over all too quickly I felt rested and refreshed and with renewed energy if somewhat apprehensive about my so-called promotion. I wondered how this assistant to Mr Keevil role would work, as I could not see myself able to cope with his job – of finding work for the gangs and billets for girls – quite apart from dealing with much administration and government regulations.

13 Travelling Supervisor
January - June 1944

WHILE AWAITING THE ISSUE OF a motorbike, my promotion only showed on my pay slip. I was now to earn £300 a year, and felt I was very well off. The girls were gratifyingly displeased that I was no longer to be in charge of their gang but when I explained I would be in Lypiatt Hostel most evenings, though out and about much of the day, they were glad they could still see me about any problems that might arise, as I would still have overall charge of gangs in the area. As my room was still a double room I shared at times with trainee forewomen I was very pleased that, on hearing of my new job, Mr Yarnold had my room changed to a single room, exchanging the spare wardrobe and chest for a desk and chair. This had a nice executive feel and quite impressed the girls.

Before a brief Christmas leave for us all, I had Miss Prentice and Miss Laws for a short training. They were good company, enjoyed being with Corsham camp and liked the camp facilities, especially the snack bar, and the weekly padre's hour. Miss Laws left Corsham abruptly to take over Enford gang, as Phyl Munro had 'flu.

On 21st December, 1943, before going home on Christmas leave, I took girls to the station, all bubbling with joy at the thought of going home for a few days. The girls from the North were facing long and slow journeys, but having company helped. I had hoped to get a bus to Bournemouth, but all the buses were overflowing, so it was another slow journey with changes and long waits, but to be home for Christmas was worth it. Sadly we received news that our twenty-one-year-old cousin Geoff, who had spent many school holidays with us over the years, had been killed serving in the R.A.F. while mine laying over Crete. It brought home to us how many were the homes that Christmas, all over the world, mourning lost family not with them for Christmas. We all received cards he had posted just before he died.

On my return I arranged a meeting with my co-supervisor Phyl in Westbury to talk over our new responsibilities. We spent the night in a little-used War Ag. property in the town. Before settling into cold damp beds a crash of breaking glass had us walking gingerly around carrying pokers, as American soldiers had been known to break in and use the house sometimes. We settled in for a restless night after barricading our doors.

Trouble awaited my return to Corsham. Miss Bristow, sent to drive half Corsham gang, had trouble getting on with Bart and Fernee and the girls. The trouble arose because Bristow thought she had charge of the gang, so I told her she was to assist Bart and Fernee. The girls were happier when this was put right, and I was thankful to be called away to open a new hostel. I was to take some girls and Miss Jones, a new forewoman, to Conock Manor the next evening. On a foggy, frosty evening, with little light from the slit in the hooded headlights, it was difficult to find our way, so, when a sizeable mansion showed up, we cheered. Unfortunately it was Urchfont Manor. A man in the grounds redirected us, and I asked if this had been the home of the Pollock family. He was interested to know I had once briefly met a son of the family, known to my sister. (He was the most handsome young man that I, then seventeen-years-old, had ever met, and I remembered he had telephoned his mother that evening at Urchfont Manor.) Fortunately we learned that Conock Manor was not far away.

Girls already in residence were happy to show my excited girls to their dormitories while I went in search of the temporary Warden, Mrs Thrussel. There were beautiful old tapestries still hanging around the magnificent large entrance hall, and lovely dark oak staircases at each end of the hall. The girls had to wear light shoes on the fine oak parquet floors. It was astonishing to think of this lovely home now in use as a hostel for Land Girls. The gang was wildly over-excited, racing about looking in and out of this vast dwelling, and

Twenty-six of the hard-working Corsham Gang:
Front row from left to right: Fay, Gang Leader, Anne Hall, Area Supervisor (the author); Mrs. Hilda Keevil, Asst. Labour Officer; The Hon. Mrs. Grace Methuen, W.L.A. Rep.; Mr Michael Culham, County Labour Officer; Suzette Nathan, Forewoman.

getting themselves lost. Despite the cold, foggy, dark evening, some found their way out to the imposing stable building in an adjoining yard. Though I did not realize it that evening, I was very annoyed to discover later that they had been in the stables and found their way up into an attractive clock turret on the stable roof. They had somehow interfered with the clock and put it out of action. This striking clock had kept very good time, and was appreciated locally as the strike could be heard for some distance, so people had come to depend on it. The Land Girls had lost no time in making themselves very unpopular with the villagers. The village had been dismayed when the Manor was requisitioned for the Army who had already caused some damage, especially to the floors, already well-pitted with heavy army boots. The girls noted this very quickly and did not see much point in them having to wear light shoes now the damage had been done. I had to sympathise with them over this, but did not alter the regulation as they might learn to appreciate the exceptional accommodation they were privileged to enjoy for a time.

In the general excitement I was quite envious of Miss Jones, as we settled comfortably in the deep window seats, each with a radiator, but the mood changed the next morning when we were faced with unhappy, homesick girls who decided they did not find this large dwelling homely. Two girls had packed up and they left after breakfast. The warden was also unhappy and wanted to leave. Fortunately, Mr Brown, Area Labour Officer, called in early to see how we were faring and he managed to calm things down. He then asked me if I could spend a weekend with Rosemary Headley, in Salisbury, as she wanted to leave her War Ag. job. I could not really spare the time. I did write to her, but she left the job shortly after. I spent the week with Miss Jones and pulled many a drill of swedes with the gang, which was working hard. On Saturday evening Mr and Mrs Keevil came to see the hostel and to bring two new girls in place of the two who had left. They stayed to tea, and Mrs Keevil invited me to spend Sunday with them. This I was delighted to accept, as I was to be back in Corsham then. I was glad to be back in 'Q' Block, though Miss Jones was not altogether happy on her own with her gang. Having been issued with my motorbike in the week, and finding it handy to get about with ease, I rode it to the Keevils' on Sunday. I arrived frozen to the eyelashes, and very wet. I quickly thawed out before their open fire, and then had a most happy day of fun and games with the three children. Bridget, the four-year-old, decided I was a good horse for her. Returning to Corsham from Chippenham through a thick cold mist I felt weary and depressed, wishing I could be with family again. I settled for early bath and bed to get warmed up.

For the next five months I was constantly on the move, visiting different hostels and often working in small threshing gangs. The girls in these gangs lived in billets; their time-keeping and standard of work was often deplorable, and needed supervision. The frequent evening visits of Michael Culham were a needed tonic – the motorcycling in winter was no joy – but he was sometimes depressingly critical of my efforts, leaving me very disheartened and depressed. It cheered me to be invited to serve on social work committees, at meetings of Labour Officers and at conferences over hostel problems. These were a pleasant break from the arduous threshing and other field work. Even so, Phyl and I often talked of giving up.

When we had first been issued with our 250cc B.S.A. motorbikes we were delighted with them. It made getting around our areas easier and quicker. They had been well used and by the time we got them they had no windscreens or leg guards. As we were not given any special clothing we bought ourselves leather helmets and fleecy-lined gauntlets. We wore our canvas uniform leggings but soon found it necessary to stuff newspaper in our socks and under our pullovers to make something of a windbreak.

It was a cold winter, and we came to hate the bike riding. In the pitch dark, on icy roads, and very often in freezing fog, it was a nightmare as the masked headlamps showed very little road ahead of us, and it was impossible to read road signs. When quite lost one morning on a very early ride to deal with a hostel dispute, riding across the lonely plains I was cheered to see a glowing brazier outside an army camp. I rode across to the guard on duty, hoping to get a 'warm up' while finding out where I was. A very large black American soldier emerged from his hut, eyes widening in fright at this tubby figure on a motor bike. Equally startled, I revved up and roared off into the dark, no doubt leaving him wondering whatever sort of apparition he had seen.

I eventually found my way to Mere hostel, so cold that my nostrils did freeze, and ice balls actually formed in my hair. I was in no mood to enjoy the laughter and merriment of the girls at the sight of me, but made my way to the warden's room to find out what her problem was, and to have a welcome warm up, and a cooked breakfast.

Social work meetings were held monthly in a hotel in Devizes. More often than not I would arrive to join Lady Catherine McNeil and Mrs Methuen, with my clothes and face coated in runny mud and with matted wet hair. A quick dash to the 'Ladies' did little to improve matters, but they were always sympathetic and understanding and not really happy about me having to travel on a motorbike so much, though it did save precious petrol.

I ordered a good pair of breeches and a Harris jacket to try to improve my image, and was horrified to be charged £15 for clothes which were really not up to the job. Moss Bros. did admit they were unhappy with the poor wartime materials and did much leather patching repairs, free of charge. When Dad heard of my extravagance, I did not receive any rebuke, but was sent a cheque for the £15.

Organising where to work each day was not an easy task. In order to check on the small threshing gangs in digs here and there, I would find out where they were working by contacting threshing contractors, and receiving reports on their work. Where girls were failing to turn up or were constantly late I would travel round to find their digs and, if there was no valid reason for their failure to work, they would be reported and lose pay, but if they had overslept they would be sent off late to work. When I heard a gang was to work at Stanton Fitzwarren, where Reg Smeeton was now farm manager, I rang up and was invited to join the gang and stay for meals and the night – an enjoyable way to catch up on one another's news. They were again feeling unsettled and wanted me to rejoin them at another farm. I felt they disapproved of my supervisor role, that I was getting 'bigheaded' and was no longer the hard-working Land Girl they had known. Maybe they were right, but I felt I was just becoming warweary, and the hard slog was taking its toll. On returning to Corsham I found Mr Culham there awaiting me and, as usual, his encouragement decided me against leaving War Ag. Even better, he had come to tell me I was to give up the motorcycling and go to Trowbridge to collect a van instead. I was very sad to learn that he was concerned about the danger involved in using these bikes because of the death of 'Paddy' whom I had met at the depot when changing bikes.

Paddy had evidently been killed leaving the depot when a military motorcyclist lost control racing round a bend and drove straight into Paddy's bike. Paddy had just told me he was applying for a van, as his wife worried about him on the bike and she was expecting their first child very shortly. I had experienced some narrow shaves and Phyl Munro narrowly escaped death when we were travelling together down a narrow lane in single file. Coming round a sharp bend we met a convoy of American lorries travelling at great speed. I drove my bike up the nearside bank, while Phyl tried to race to the other side of the road as the Yanks were taking up all the lane. The front lorry hit the back of Phyl's bike, and she was flung headlong into a deep ditch. Not a single lorry in the convoy stopped, so apparently drivers were too high up to see our bikes. I could not get across to Phyl until all the lorries had passed. How relieved I was, on reaching her, to hear a flow of impolite language issuing from the ditch, and to see Phyl well covered in runny mud, but recovering amazingly well from the shock. The soft mud must have saved her any injury. The news that we would be spared further motorcycling was welcome indeed, but how sad that it took Paddy's death to come to this decision. Michael Culham said he would never forgive himself if we were hurt riding bikes, and vans were on order.

On the whole it was a good feeling to be back in Corsham, in my own room and with my own girls, and to have the ready help and advice of Mr Keevil. I was rarely able to stay long and this visit, as it turned out, was no exception. I found Miss Hobday overjoyed at having been allowed to have a total immersion Baptism at the Baptist church, despite anxiety that she suffered from a heart complaint. I went with her to an inspiring Padre's Hour, and gleaned local news.

I was pleased to receive an invitation from Culham to attend the interviewing of prospective WLA Forewomen. I felt I now knew pretty well the qualities required for this work. I was always surprised at the varied experiences of life in the WLA and I very much enjoyed meeting these candidates. I was not so pleased when I received a sudden summons from Trowbridge to pack up and leave Corsham and to take Vera Long with me to open up a Volunteer Harvest Camp in farm buildings at Mr Jeffrey's farm in Donhead St. Mary. We were to set off the next day, and would have Mrs Anderson to instruct us how to set about turning the farm buildings into adequate accommodation for twenty to forty men and women who were prepared to give up holidays to help on the land.

14 Volunteer Agricultural Camp, Donhead St. Mary

June - July 1944

AFTER A BUSY TIME PACKING up and leaving Corsham and visiting Trowbridge to collect another lorry for the Camp, Vera and I eventually arrived at the Donhead farm. Mrs Anderson was there to outline the great amount of work to be done in forty-eight hours – a barn and a large shed must be transformed into male and female dormitories, and pig pens were to be equipped as wash and shower rooms. Another stone-built barn, with an adjoining room, was to become the dining room and kitchen; a low window between them would act as a serving hatch. Our job was to scrub floors and walls, and then to erect the camp beds and put four folded blankets and a pillow on each bed, as soon as these provisions arrived from Trowbridge. Feeling already quite tired it looked a daunting prospect and one we were not wildly enthusiastic about. Mrs Anderson assessed our mood and very kindly drove us to Westbury to enjoy a meal, and to spend the night there in the War Ag. House.

Arriving back in Shaftesbury, we helped 'Andy' with a load of shopping and ordering of supplies for the Camp and got stuck into the necessary hard work at the camp. We had to break off to join a meeting in Trowbridge, convened by Culham, outlining the duties of Labour Officers and Forewomen at these Camps. Culham then came to see the Donhead site, a delay we could have well done without.

By the next evening Vera and I felt we had done at least a week's work in twenty-four hours, but 'Andy' was far from satisfied with our efforts and worried that we were nowhere near ready for the volunteers already awaiting collection at Shaftesbury station.

Vera Long (Shortie), with lorry 'Emma', Donhead Camp.

Those first forty volunteers were a grand lot and, far from complaining, enjoyed giving us lots of help in making the camp as attractive and comfortable as possible. The women and girls approved the work we had done in the former granary, transforming it into a reasonable dormitory. Some of the men helped to colourwash the dining room walls, and wash down the newly-converted washrooms, even after a day of farm work. I was envious of Vera being given the job of driving the volunteers to the farms, while I kept the kitchen stove going with much wood cutting, and prepared vast quantities of vegetables needed for the evening meal. The married couple, Mr and Mrs Bannister, engaged as cooks, had already had had enough of camp life and wanted to leave, but Andy persuaded them to stay while she tried to get new volunteers for the job.

In the evening I enjoyed the campers' company and was delighted to recognise a former friend from Bournemouth, whom I used to meet when hiking with the International Friendship League.

Entertainment in free hours for campers was not always easy, but a visit to a village pub pleased most campers, as a chance to meet the villagers. I used to ring round the local pubs during the day to see which, if any, had supplies of beer or cider, in order to know which pub to visit. We often met the Vicar where the beer was, not because he wanted the drink, but he helped behind the bar and met farmers and others who rarely attended church. He told me he learned more of their anxieties and problems this way, and it was not easy to find them at home in working hours. Some of the campers were adept at arranging good home-spun entertainment in camp, revealing quite a lot of unsuspected talent. Vera and I could never get to bed until the campers had all settled, as there was always clearing up to do, and the tables had to be set for breakfast.

On the memorable night of 6th June, as Vera and I were making our way across to the women's dormitory, there was a great roar of planes filling the sky in very close formation and all brightly lit up. We cheered and waved and roused the campers to come out to see the sight, as this surely must mean Germany was to be invaded at last. All weariness was forgotten as we rejoiced. I am sure that all the prayers and thoughts that night went with the invading soldiers and Air Force support. Could these dark days of war really be coming to an end? Surely they could.

The next morning I took the campers to work as Vera was taken by the Labour Officer to visit farms in a search for more work for the volunteers. We had to chop down gorse on rough sloping ground that was to be reclaimed for pasture. I was working with Mrs Willoughby, a gynaecologist, who proved very effective at wielding a chopper, and we made speedy progress and became good friends by the end of the day. She seemed to love the camp life and work and stayed a second week. She cheered the new cooks by her ready appreciation of all they served. We never enjoyed seeing the campers back to the station just as we had got to know them and, for a day or two, it was not easy to feel as much for the new crowd, but they all quickly became our family again. Someone gave the press an encouraging write-up on the camp, and we never discovered who it was, but it cheered us on when we were finding the long hours very tiring.

Vera and I quite fell for a very helpful camper who was employed near Salisbury, and visited the camp several times after he had left. Vera and this camper, Paul David, became engaged for a time, and I was quite sad when Vera changed her mind and we heard no more of that very nice man who had proved such a good friend. Paul was replaced as a great helper by Dave Brockett, a Glaswegian, who was in no hurry to leave camp. 'Jock', as Dave was known to all, told me he was not happy about the engineering work he did in Glasgow, as it affected his health. He was held there under an 'Essential Work' order, and the only way he could get a change of work was to stay away until discharged for 'gross misconduct'. Mr Culham agreed to me taking him on as paid camp staff, as he was very useful around the camp.

Jock was popular with the campers, and useful in dealing with male campers who were a bit awkward at times. On one occasion a group of students ignored the warning to go easy on the cider at the local, as Wiltshire cider was quite potent. When I collected these lads, I had an anxious time driving home, as they were chasing each other round the back of the lorry wielding reaping hooks. The Vicar had warned me they had had rather too much cider and had helped to load them into the lorry. As soon as I got to camp, Jock took command and they were taken to the men's showers and deluged with cold water until sobered up. They spent the evening coming to me and apologising over and over again, until Jock persuaded them off to bed.

When Jock dropped a brick on a string down the flue while cleaning the kitchen stove chimney, the result was the kitchen being covered in soot. The students made up for their lapse in behaviour by cleaning it up and redecorating. The dining room also was given a fresh colourwash and, when Vera came along with lots of sweet peas to decorate the tables, the room was much more inviting than the barn as we first saw it. Culham was quite impressed when he

Holiday volunteer farm workers.

turned up unexpectedly. I was led across to his car for a chat and was told I was shortly to return to Corsham to run another volunteer camp, to be housed in Nissen huts, which had been vacated by an army searchlight party. I was advised to find campers in Donhead willing to help me in Corsham. I said I might persuade a New Zealand authoress who wanted a long spell in camp to accompany me, and Jock would very likely agree to help. Michael said I could employ both if willing to move. He then went on to say he was seeking other work, and wondered if I would be willing to go with him. I was not happy to hear he was likely to leave the War Ag. but could not say I would go with him unless I had some idea of what work he was likely to move to. I did not think I would be so happy in the War Ag. employ with a different boss since Michael and I got on very easily, despite the lectures I received from time to time when my work was not considered good enough. I could not quite understand why he should want me to work with him since he did not seem to know himself what the work was likely to be.

In my drowsy state at the end of the day, sitting in the car in the dusk with this young man, I could have been tempted to wonder if this was the beginning of a fine romance. Michael was held in high regard by all the Labour Officers who appreciated that he worked hard yet created a family feeling amongst his colleagues, and inspired us all to give of our best, though we were made to work hard for long hours, because *he* was such a worker. Did he really appreciate my work, or were personal feelings involved? Ours was always a strictly businesslike relationship, though we got on well. I was too sleepy to give it much thought, but hoped he was not soon to leave his job. Meanwhile I had better concentrate on getting organised for the next move. I would be sorry to lose Vera's company and help. She got on wonderfully well with all the campers, and I doubted if I would succeed as well at Corsham without her. I would now be quite sorry to leave this somewhat primitive camp as the hardships seemed to generate a wonderful spirit amongst the campers. Despite our dismay when first seeing the farm facilities, or lack of them, we had grown to enjoy the way it had been developed. I was thankful to see Michael off and to get to bed and immediately fall sound asleep.

15 Ladbrook Volunteer Agricultural Camp, Corsham

July 1944

On 26th July, 1944, Irene Adcock – 'Mopsy' – authoress from New Zealand, was helping me to load our luggage in the van when one of the Campers came to give me a farewell present of £3 from the week's volunteers, with a card of good wishes for the start of the new camp. This kindness made me even more reluctant to leave a camp where I now felt so much at home. I was glad to have Mopsy's company as we faced the challenge ahead, of having very little time to transform an army searchlight camp of Nissen huts into a comfortable, smooth-running camp for up to ninety volunteers a week. As we set off to collect a lorry from the transport depot in Trowbridge, Jock assured me he would soon be following me to Corsham to join my staff. A cheering thought, as Jock was very well-liked around camp, and a great worker.

We found our camp off the Lacock road out of Corsham, down a pleasant lane. After passing a small chapel in a burial ground, lined by an imposing row of tall poplars, we came to the Nissen huts in fields either side of the lane. Up a slope on the left was the entrance to a large tarmac lorry park, and opposite was the Nissen hut which was to be my HQ, standing alone, set in a field of wheat. It was a very rural spot, and we were glad to note a farmhouse a little way up the lane.

Across the lane opposite my hut was the dining hut, facing the cookhouse. Behind the dining hut were two Nissen huts, one a recreation room, and one that was to become the women's dormitory. Down a twisty narrow path at the side of a pasture field, some hundred yards or so, were two washroom huts fitted with basins, baths and shower units. Below these were two more huts (with Elsan buckets) for use as Ladies and Gents WCs. (It would take a brave soul to trek down this narrow path in the dark.) We went back across the lane to inspect two huts at the far end of the corn field – another tidy trek. These were the men's dormitories, well away from the ladies' quarters. We found Rose, a Londoner, whom I was told would be our helper on our arrival. Rose was setting up forty- five camp beds, and supplying each with four folded army blankets. It was suggested we might like to start doing the same for the ladies' dorm., but I decided we would eat first, to rest from our travels. While enjoying the supper Rose had prepared, we learnt that Rose was unlikely to be with us long. Country life was foreign to her and she found the silence, only interrupted by animal and bird noises, very frightening, especially the eerie sound of the many owls at night. She was thankful to have our company and glad that 'Mopsy' would share her hut that night.

When Mopsy and I had got the women's dormitory to our satisfaction, we decided to make for bed early. Mopsy realised she would have to get used to the large army-issue, black lead, coal-burning stove in the cookhouse in the morning, before having to cook for the camp, so wanted to be up early, and to estimate what supplies would be needed for breakfasts, picnic lunches and hot drinks for the evening. The main evening meal would be supplied daily from the schools catering service. I would have to get in touch with Mr Keevil to know what work was to be available for volunteers and to find out if I was needed to help with Corsham WLA gang as well, as I was still their senior Forewoman and on call if needed.

As we went to our huts and to our narrow bunks with 'the rough male kiss' of army blankets, Rose warned me to lock the doors each end of the hut, as the 'Searchlight lads' had not all left camp, and I might hear cars driving on to the car park in the night. Finding that the phone in my office was working, I telephoned Michael Culham right away to ask if he could arrange a speedy withdrawal of the soldiers, since I would be meeting the first volunteers the next day.

Farm Activities:

Sowing

Harvesting

Threshing from farmyard barns

Opening a potato clamp

He seemed concerned, so I assured him they were keeping to themselves in tents at the bottom of the field and would be no worry to us.

Suddenly awakened from a deep sleep, I was aware of the slamming of a car door, and footsteps coming towards the gate to my cornfield. I shot off the bunk, snatched at my dressing gown and slippers and was relieved to see the familiar figure of Michael Culham. I stepped out of the hut to find he had come to make sure we were not troubled by the soldiers. Michael always worked very long hours so it was nothing unusual for him to appear after midnight. It was a lovely full moon and it could have been quite romantic, listening to the breeze rustling in the standing corn, but it always seemed to be my luck to have these moments with very distant men. I took the opportunity, however, to ask my charming boss if he could arrange for the camp to be supplied with mats to cover some of the concrete floors, and perhaps some comfortable chairs in the recreation room, and to this he agreed. Though I was ready to resume sleep Michael seemed reluctant to leave, so we talked on for half an hour or so before he drove off into the night. As stillness descended, I found I was now wide awake enough to start worrying about the new responsibilities thrust upon me. I lay trying to work out the sort of routine my work would now demand.

As Camp Supervisor I would have a lot more duties and responsibilities than I had had at Mere. The days would be very long, probably starting sometimes at 4.30 am when 'early bird' farmers would ring up with last minute requests for labour when the weather was right for harvest, and I would have to get parties of friends sorted out to work together on the jobs they preferred. I would have to get them to the lorry at the time it was going to the area in which they were to work, and I would have to do at least three trips to get all the campers to work. I would have to sort out the parties at breakfast when all would be assembled and hope to get something to eat when they were at work. Mopsy would require daily shopping, and that would take much of the rest of the morning. There were reports to write on campers and work, and entertainments to arrange for the evenings. As at last I drifted off to sleep I decided I would clearly need more help. It seemed no time until I was rudely awoken by a shrill alarm.

The first week was quite chaotic, as much still needed doing to make camp reasonably comfortable. Although Rose did stay awhile, it was clear from the start that she and Mopsy would not work happily as a team, and I must keep my eye open for a replacement. Our very first volunteers arrived when Mopsy and I were just about to carry the Elsan buckets down to the bottom field. These two young men were somewhat surprised and amused to find that we were Supervisor and Cook, respectively. They took over at once the job of setting up the lavatories. In no time at all Mopsy and I were surrounded with charming volunteers adopting the camp as home, and undertaking every possible job – handymen and women everywhere giving finishing touches. It was a wonderful experience for Mopsy and me to see people from all walks of life, and from all over the country, arrive as complete strangers yet so quickly becoming one joyful family. One of the heart-warming aspects of a dreadful war was the way it brought down barriers – all pulled together so happily to do anything to help bring the war to a successful end and to see peace and freedom restored.

I had received from County Hall lists of rules and regulations as to how the camp should be run. At first reading I was a bit bothered as to how I, at twenty-four-years of age, was to keep volunteers to these rules. (Imagine telling a high ranking officer he must be in by 10 pm!) So far, the majority of the campers were older and far more worldly-wise than me. I quickly decided to have no rules, so they went into the wastepaper basket and were never missed. (I heard later that my camp was the only one that kept going into October because it was the one without any rules.)

16 Camp Supervisor

July - November 1944

IN OUR FIRST WEEK ALL age groups were represented and worked well together. Mr and Mrs Bevan and their daughter, a very pleasant family; a Yorkshire Scout, Joe Butterworth; Peter and Charlie from London; Mr Byfield and Miss Lovett, an engaged couple; four lively lads – Miller, Brooker, Pollard and Scott; the quiet Mr McIntyre; and two older men, Mr Gamlin and Mr Hardman, were soon all known to us by their readiness to help in any way. It was encouraging when Mr Luetchford and Mr Wood and friends decided to book in for a further week.

Early on, a German school teacher decided to stay almost to the end of camp. We were glad to enrol him as staff. This, however, upset Fred, who was already helping in the cookhouse. Fred had served in the Navy for sixteen years, and was a very good worker, but stone deaf as a result of having manned the naval guns. He soon took exception to the way Mopsy fussed over Michael, a German Jew. Mopsy felt sad for Michael having been forced to leave his home and family as a boy of fourteen, to escape the Nazis. His parents were now in Australia and his brother in America and, not being too welcome elsewhere, Michael was in camp for the holiday. He was given English nationality, and changed his name from Buchdahl to Buckdale, so Fred's attitude was unreasonable, if understandable.

It was not easy to reason with Fred, of course, because we had to write our remarks, as he was so deaf. Fred was a very efficient worker, but Mopsy found the discord too much, while she was so busy, so Fred had to go, and was replaced by another Michael, an Irish lad who stayed to the end of the camp.

Mopsy's husband Cyril, who was at college in England, and their

Michael Buckdale.

two daughters, Fleur and Marilyn, would come and spend a week in camp whenever free and seemed to enjoy the company.

Other visitors included some of the searchlight men, who still were in camp nearby. They liked to drop in to the cookhouse for a cuppa, and were very good at helping at evening entertainments. I was often driving volunteers to Bath in the evening, or to Chippenham, to attend pictures or a dance or, if lucky, they might find a pub which had some beer. This made for a long working day and, at the end of it, Michael Culham and Bob Hardy found that they could get late refreshments at Ladbrook, sometimes when we had just got the campers out of the cookhouse and were hoping to get to bed. They were always full of energy, and really enjoyed the informal camp life and were in no hurry to leave. They were good company however, and it was good to meet them in an informal way, so we made no protest. It was the only form of relaxation we got. Mopsy was well-placed for getting regular meals but I never found it easy to stop to eat, though I would often find a plate of toast on the bonnet of the lorry, as Mopsy was concerned that I was not getting enough food while always on the go and constantly on call.

The long hours were tiring but, perhaps more demanding for a twenty-four-year-old was having to deal with many different temperaments and maintaining a harmonious atmosphere, as these people were supposed to be having a much-needed holiday from their war work. Organising working parties sometimes involved sending people to work that did not appeal to them, and though most took this in good part there were those who thought they were not being treated as fairly as others whose work sounded more attractive. This needed tactful handling, but I got help with this. Michael Culham allowed me to employ my sister and her school friend, in the long school summer holidays, and they took on this role of getting the parties organised and to the lorry at the right time. Jill and friend June made very good co-hostesses, and got to know all the volunteers which was helpful to me, as I had little chance of knowing more than a few, each week, though I had to make a brief report on each. The girls could help me with those I did not really know. Farmers also had to be kept happy, and not all the volunteers were able to put in as good a day's work as farmers hoped, and unless they were pleased it was not easy to continue to get work for volunteers.

One Sunday morning I received a last minute call from a nearby farm for a few volunteers to help clear a field of corn, as the weather and crop were just right. Without knowing any of the volunteers I took the first eight to respond. Unfortunately none had had any such experience, and though game to learn, were not a lot of help as they needed supervising. One man, trying to pick up a sheaf from under a horse, did not get the sheaf properly on the fork and stabbed the horse's belly as he lifted it. Not only did the horse rear and then bolt, but he smashed his way out of a costly harness, not easy to repair or replace, and the horse would be nervous of settling to that work again for a time. There was no consoling the farmer, and the volunteers were somewhat upset at all being sent back to camp at once. No more volunteers were requested by that farmer. Fortunately, it was the only incident of its kind. Many farmers sent me letters of great appreciation for the work of novices, and continued to offer work of all sorts, and were thankful for the way these good people gave holiday time to try to help. I was always glad to send on these letters to Trowbridge. The Corsham WLA girls sometimes worked alongside the volunteers and helped them by showing them how best to do the given job.

Every Saturday saw us taking to the station all our new friends and enduring sad partings. At the same time we returned to camp feeling rather depressed, with a load of strangers, which we thought could never be as nice as our last week's campers, but of course they quickly became just as much fun. There was an outstanding week that was most memorable. Jock had rejoined us by this time, and was loved by all campers, especially at our home entertainment evening when he always responded to the request to sing 'I belong to Glasgow' (in fact his home town).

Ladbrook volunteers assisted by Corsham Gang.

Jock had a lovely voice and the right accent, so this was appreciated and all left with a great affection for him. I found Jock a tower of strength helping to run the men's side of camp life, and keeping order in the men's quarters. Not only so, but Jock was always concerned that my strength would possibly be overtaxed. On Saturdays, when we had dances at Lypiatt to attend, many volunteers would feel it right to ask me to dance, though I really lacked the energy to accept many such kind offers. After a few dances, Jock would lead me on to the floor every time a man seemed to be coming my way.

After a few steps we would then go and sit out, and in this way I was able to relax without giving offence by refusing dances.

In that special week we had a lot of lively college students. County Hall, Trowbridge, evidently decided to mix the nationalities in my camp during that week. Amongst the usual English volunteers from different walks of life, including four very lively Birmingham college volunteers, there arrived first a Persian – Eprime Eschag. A young Polish man who spoke no English then arrived carrying a very large radio; some thought he was using this to transmit messages but, as we could not communicate with this Michael, his visit was a bit of a mystery. He came and went several times during the week and did not take on much work. A charming young Chinese student was at once very popular and all the farmers asked for his help as he proved to be a very efficient worker. Chiu Ban Yt, I learned (as much of his mail came from religious sources), was a Cambridge student studying theology, with a view to entering the Church. He was keen that I did not spread the news as he did not want volunteers to treat him as a clergyman in camp. 'Bunny', as he was called, proved to be in demand at dances, as the girls told me he was expert at dancing the rumba. (Many years later I recognised 'Bunny' on television, walking in a procession of bishops at a Lambeth conference, and learned he was then Bishop of Singapore. We met again at a conference when he was retired and he still recalled the backache he suffered after much potato picking!)

A Russian international lawyer also joined us that week. Marc Wilenkin was a little distressed at Eprime's irrepressible teasing, and I had to rebuke Eprime and appeal to him to consider Marc's sensitivity, but for the rest it was a week of great fun for all. There was much ragging between the Birmingham students and Jock, whom they singled out for many practical jokes to which Jock responded well. Then, one day, he treated them to apple pie and custard with a nice layer of mustard powder under the custard, to the delight of the other campers. There were very good University type debates on wet days in which all took part. Eprime's proposal 'That a system

115

My motorbike centre of attention.

One of the Ladbrook families.

of Rational Morality should replace world religions to spare us much hostility and even wars,' provoked a most interesting and lively debate enjoyed by all. I was interested to note what a lot of keen Christians we had in Camp, who came out in strong opposition to the proposal. It created great fellowship amongst these for the rest of the week.

When that week ended Mopsy and I felt very flat, and began to weary of the pace of Camp life. It was not unusual for campers to arrive at all times in the night and, after one night when I had to take the lorry to meet some at midnight and the 1.15 am, I also got a call to go to Chippenham at 4.45 am for another six just arriving. That happened to be on a day when I had been instructed to lead a convoy of American trucks which had volunteered to help convey Land Girls to a rally. We were to collect gangs from Corsham, then Little Somerford at 8.30 am, and finally Lavington and Ashton Keynes, and take them to a gathering near Savernake. The gathering gave the Forewomen a chance to get together while the rally was on and to have a bit of a moan about our various hardships. After the hundred and seventy miles or so of motoring, with the constant whine of the American trucks as well as our own noisy lorries, I had an outsize in headaches and was glad to get back to the kindly Mopsy giving me an excellent meal to cheer me on. I then felt so much better I accompanied Mopsy to Evensong, as I suddenly remembered it was Sunday, so we had not to take the volunteers out for entertainment.

The Harvest Camps closed down in October but, though most were closed early in the month, Ladbrook kept open until early November as so many volunteers came back for a further week. Despite all the hard work, it was a depressing business dismantling Camp. It had been a wonderful experience and I had had a marvellous team, who gave all they had got to making the Camp a joyful time for all. Camp had become home for a varied and happy large family, and the prospect of returning to hostels and digs as Forewoman once more, was not a thought that brought much comfort.

In my sober mood I was cheered on greatly by a R.E.M.E. soldier,

Mick, R.E.M.E. Camp helper.

Mick, who had adopted Ladbrook as a second home, almost as soon as the Camp opened, spending all free evenings and days off with us, making himself very useful in any way that offered. He was as sad as we were to see Camp close, but he was a tower of strength to us in our efforts to dismantle. One by one the team departed, and only Jock and Mick remained to help with the folding of beds and bedding, packing up all the huts, and sweeping all those concrete floors, without much in the way of damp tealeaves now to settle the dust. With very heavy hearts we said our farewells – Mick off back to his Camp and Jock to a job in Trowbridge to service tractors for the War Ag., since he could not return to his former work in Glasgow. It felt a real bereavement to me as I finally turned the key to my Nissen hut office, set in the silence of that farm field, no longer adorned by corn, but so peaceful and silent.

Reporting to Michael Culham in County Hall, my sense of humour was not uppermost, and I failed to note the joke when he said I was looking so fit after my holiday at Camp he would like me to forego the leave he had offered me (because my Mother was about to undergo an operation). Before I exploded, he hastily assured me it was a joke and he did much appreciate the work I had done, and I was to take two weeks, not one. I was indeed thankful for this, and relaxed.

I wanted to ask Michael if there was any substance in the rumour that he was about to leave the War Ag., but he got in first by accusing me of getting restless, and talking of leaving. It was true all of us were beginning to look to the end of the war, and wondering what work we should be seeking. Some of the men were beginning to return to the land and our role could not last much longer. Michael assured me I would not lose my job with the War Ag.; in fact I was to return from leave as an assistant Labour Officer, working in Mr Keevil's area. This reassured me that Michael was not likely to be leaving or he would probably have told me of his plans.

I was ready to get away for my two weeks at home and, though I was to do some housekeeping while Mother was undergoing her operation, this prospect sounded like a rest cure after camp life. I had had very little time to communicate with home during Camp, but Mother had been to stay at Ladbrook for a week and enjoyed the views of beautiful Wiltshire from the lorry cab, but we still had lots of chat to make up. I was given permission to ride my motor bike to the Salisbury depot and to catch a bus to Bournemouth, in order to avoid a slow train journey. By 5 pm I was at home once more, but feeling a bit lost without Camp and my colleagues and campers.

17　Labour Officer Assistant

November 1944 - January 1946

THE TWO WEEKS OF HOME life went all too quickly, but a spell of domestic work while Mother recovered from her operation gave me time to talk over future plans. Like Michael Culham, Dad thought I would be wise to leave the land and train for social work, as my experience of working with so many Campers from all walks of life, and of all ages, would be a valuable commendation. I felt I would be happier running my own smallholding, but lacked the necessary funds for such an enterprise. My friends in War Ag. were already leaving to return to 'Civvy Street' – Sue Nathan returning to Reading University to complete her degree course, interrupted by the war; Ursula Russell thinking of training in hotel management; Phyl Munro had gone to take up work as a farm secretary, and Vera Long, now engaged to our Donhead camper, Paul David, was likely to return to her Bank of England job. It was all very unsettling, and I felt it was more than likely Michael Culham was also looking for other work. The idea of being assistant to Mr Keevil, while offering a rise in salary and a promotion, was not as much my cup of tea, I felt, as being Supervisor of hostel and Forewoman of W.L.A. gangs, a role I enjoyed, but I wondered how long it would be likely to last.

Arriving back in Trowbridge, on 27th November 1944, having been seen off on the bus by Mother, in rather watery sunshine, and having enjoyed the journey through the country areas all looking lovely after rain, the day continued happily as Michael gave me a warm welcome back. He drove me round to the transport depot to enjoy my delight at being given a brand new Hillman van, which had been set aside for me. I was to work from Chippenham office, but it was suggested I should look for digs in Swindon, as much of the work would be in that area. Poor Mr Keevil was laid up with a nasty dose of mumps, so no sooner did I enter the Chippenham office than I was swamped with work – bikes to be taken to hostels, digs to be found for local Land Girls, landladies to be encouraged to keep girls, etc. I was thankful eventually to get on to Lypiatt, and to be welcomed by the gang, most of whom I still knew.

On Wednesday I found myself comfortable digs at 92, Rodbourne Road with Fred and Dot Chandler, who were very welcoming. I decided to move in with them on December 4th, the next Monday. I kept my room at Lypiatt also, as I would still be needed by gangs in Corsham area at times. Work was not so very different, as much of the day was still spent with gangs, but I was conscious that my relationship with the Labour Officers was more strained, and I was made to feel that Mr Keevil certainly had no need of an assistant and thought I was not much good either at finding digs or work for the area, so I found myself often sent to work with the small gangs, most of whom lived in digs and were a bit slack at getting to work on time.

By the end of December I was quite sure I ought to look around for other work. I felt I was idling along trying to fill a role that really did not exist. When Michael Culham arrived one evening I told him how I felt about my new role, and he did then admit that Mr Keevil was upset at my appointment, and felt I was perhaps being trained to take over his job. I could not believe this, that once again I was thought to be trying to oust my boss. I nearly resigned on the spot, as I had a very high regard for Mr Keevil and was well aware that I could not possibly do his work. Michael assured me he had made it clear to Mr Keevil that there was no such intention, that Mr Keevil carried such a work load he would be able to pass some of the jobs on to me. After this session the friendly relationship with Mr Keevil was restored and he understood my feelings of being somewhat 'at sea' in my role as his assistant.

I spent a happy Christmas at home, and returned feeling a lot less tired, and ready to get on with whatever work came my way from Mr Keevil, and to let the future take care of itself. A great uplift at the time was the friendship of some of the Campers who kept in touch. Peter Parkyn, a young man working in the Admiralty Offices in Bath, who had been at the Donhead and Corsham Camps, several times invited me to concerts or ballet in Bath. Sometimes at weekends we had delightful walks on the heights overlooking Bath. I was invited to tea by his Aunts who lived in the town. Peter did a lot to keep up my morale and I enjoyed his company, though this was a very platonic friendship, and the Land Girls thought it very funny when they saw me taking farewell of Peter at the station one evening, just shaking hands – they had more affectionate farewells from their soldier friends.

Michael Buckdale became a great friend for seven years, until he set sail for Australia to join his widowed mother. The Birmingham students also used to pay return visits, and this helped the winter along despite the unsettling effect of others leaving. Bart and Fernee had now left Corsham gang to work on private farms, and this led to their eventual marriages to farmers. I began to think theirs a nice means of solving what to do in the future, but the right proposal seemed a long time coming.

With the spring came that longed for day of delirious excitement for us all, May 8th, our day of Victory over Europe. That wonderful voice of Winston Churchill, which had kept us going through the long dark years, now declared that the Germans had surrendered and the war in Europe was over. I was working, at the time, with the Enford gang, and I rang Mr Hardy and was given permission to give the gang the day off to celebrate. Most of us at once made for home. At Salisbury I was lucky to catch a Bournemouth bus, and the impatience I suffered while the driver and conductor left the bus for ten minutes in Fordingbridge quickly faded. They returned with lots of bunting and flags and we passengers were able to help them to dress up the bus for our triumphant ride home. There were no police stopping us this time to see our Identity Cards to ensure we had a Bournemouth address. As soon as I got home, I rummaged around in the attic, and found the Union Flag my Granpa had flown at the end of the First

World War. We had a flagpole in the front garden, and no sooner was the flag flying than folk all up and down the Avenue were hard at it, decorating homes with lots of bunting.

Mother came with us into Bournemouth where the assembling crowds were dancing in the streets and generally going mad with joy. This was a second time round of this sort of celebration for Granny and Mother's generations. While in Meyrick Park, Churchill's announcement of the Victory over tannoys was greeted with much cheering. Returning to Southbourne, we went to All Saints Church for the service of Thanksgiving, and returned home to hear the broadcast of our beloved King of whom we were so proud for staying in England with his people. As we hastily stood for the playing of the National Anthem, one could almost feel the warmth from the glow of patriotic fervour surrounding us.

Off back to Enford and no fear of any night raids to disturb the journey. The next day was a hastily arranged Victory parade in Corsham, which I attended with the gang. The gang turned out in smart array and in good numbers. Placed well up in the parade, they were very annoyed when a Major came and made us go to the back of the procession with the Scouts and Guides, as we were only civilians. It was as well he did not hear the uncivil language about Army Majors. It spoilt the day for the girls and they wished they had not bothered to attend. Churchill came to relieve the gloom with a wonderful speech of praise for all in another broadcast that evening, making the little local parade fade into insignificance.

That weekend, Peter and I had a walk up the hill overlooking Bath. When we returned to the train we were thrilled to look over the city at dusk with lights shining from all the shops and houses. No more blacking out of windows, no more headlamp masks on cars; town and street names could return, and church bells be heard again. Men were being demobbed in ever-increasing numbers.

In July Michael asked me to run another Volunteer Agricultural Camp, but not at Ladbrook. I was to have two blocks in the Thorney Pitts Hostel, which was one of the Ministry of Labour hostels like

Lypiatt, but catered for professional workers. This did not appeal to me as a Camp, but the usual facilities were more civilised, which would appeal to some, and meals could be provided in the canteen. This had none of the crazy camp atmosphere of Ladbrook, and many of my former campers went to more rural camps. My sister Jill and her friend June came to help and, to their amusement and to the amusement of the campers, occupied cubicles labelled Matrons A and B. The camp soon filled and we were kept busy and, of course, made good friends. Peter Parkyn came to the camp when free, which was cheering, and Jill persuaded a former friend of hers in Bournemouth, Patrick Davy, to come.

Patrick had stayed at a guest house run by the mother of one of Jill's school friends, and they both enjoyed trying to plague the life out of this handsome young bank clerk who was seven or eight years older than them. Patrick enjoyed their larking and was very kind to them, and I got to know him slightly having to go and collect Jill to return home for tea. When he heard that I had a love of horses, he took me along with him to a riding lesson on Hengistbury Head. He had thought of joining the Indian Army. Unfortunately for Pat, he found himself in the British Army at the outbreak of war, and was taken prisoner-of-war at Dunkirk. Jill sent me his address as she was trying to get all his friends writing to him. I did try to keep up some correspondence but censors often returned my attempts covered in blue pencil, because I had mentioned the weather, or made some comment on food production. Some letters did get through however, and I got a very occasional card from Pat.

I was delighted to know Pat was safely home. He was looking for a way back into English life and customs after six long years in unfriendly German custody and it was not an easy time for him but Camp life, and being amongst campers constantly coming and going, seemed to be a help. I felt Pat was almost family, as he knew my home and family from pre-war days, and from the word go we got on well and enjoyed going around and working together.

I was, even so, taken by surprise when Peter Parkyn was disapproving of this, and issued an ultimatum, to the effect that if I was going to spend so much time with Pat, then he would leave camp and I would not be hearing from him or seeing him again. I tried to make Peter understand that Pat needed help to return to normal life after his traumatic years of prison camp, but Peter left camp and I neither saw him nor heard from him again. It saddened me that I must have let him down by not realising he apparently hoped for more from our friendship than I realised, as I had simply seen him as a good friend.

Patrick Davy (right) at work.

Michael Culham occasionally looked in to see how camp life was going, and took me one evening to see Netherhampton Camp where he was trying to settle a domestic issue between supervisor and staff. After sorting out the problem, I left Michael with the staff while I went to join the campers at their dance. I was delighted to find lots of my former Ladbrook campers there, including the Birmingham students, so I was not short of dance partners and was well entertained until midnight, when Michael was ready to return me to Corsham. I did not arrive back until 3 am as Michael stopped to assist motorists involved in an accident and reported the accident to a police station. To work with Michael was always full of surprises.

I often returned to camp late as I quite often used my room at Lypiatt as my office, and I could then be available to Corsham gang, who sometimes worked with the volunteers. I did not like returning to camp to find sailors at almost all the windows of the girls' block. I asked Jill and June to try to have a word with any officers they saw walking through our blocks, as the adjoining blocks were part of a land Naval training station, HMS Arthur. After a bit of ragging with a few Officers the girls were promised there would be a picket in future to keep sailors away from the camp, though they would have thought that all the nice girls loved sailors! Very soon afterwards the Corsham papers were full of the news of the engagement of Prince Philip to Princess Elizabeth and with pictures of the Prince in Corsham, as he was stationed at this Naval base. Jill and June were quite sure they then recognised Prince Philip as one of the Officers to whom they had been talking. When the Camp closed in September I felt no regret this time, and the girls found it all an anti-climax after the fun they had enjoyed at Ladbrook, though there was an outstanding day of excitement on 15th August, when we celebrated Victory over Japan.

I was in the canteen when the news was relayed that the war was really over, and the Japanese had surrendered to the Allies. The Canteen erupted into loud cheers, and I raced around the camp to say there would be no work but that the lorry would be going into Bath after I had looked in at County Hall, Trowbridge. I had to take in the Volunteers' board money. Some of the County Hall staff asked if they could travel down to the Red Lion with us, for a celebration drink. There was much merriment in the pub as a party of RAF officers was tossing one of their number up to the roof and back. Years later I was to learn that that RAF Pilot was none other than my cousin John Hall, but I failed to recognise him while he was being thrown about, and had no idea he was stationed nearby.

In Bath the volunteers scattered and agreed to find their own way back to Camp as the streets were packed and we would never keep together. Pat and I got on to a slow moving lorry trying to get through the crowds and were soon dancing in a park to a lively band along with hundreds of others. When exhausted we made our way to the Abbey gardens, and I left Patrick dozing on the grass while I went to a Service of Thanksgiving in the Abbey, attended by many servicemen and civic dignitaries. During the evening, crowds gathered in the Abbey courtyard, and we joined in the Hokey Cokey, Boomps-a-Daisy, the Lambeth Walk, the Conga and so on. Around about 10 pm I overheard it said that vehicles in the lorry park, near the canal, were being thrown into the canal by merry makers. Pat and I quickly made our way back to our lorry parked there and met up with a few volunteers on the way, who were glad to return with us to Camp while the lorry was safe.

Despite the excitement of the day, or because of it, Pat and I decided to simmer down by taking a leisurely walk in the quiet of the countryside, after the hectic and noisy scenes in Bath. We tried to imagine adjusting to life without war once more. Pat's thoughts were very much with comrades he had lost, or just lost touch with, who had meant a lot to him in his very dark days, and he still worried lest some had not survived. The little he mentioned to me that evening about some of the atrocities and horrors experienced in imprisonment shook me to the core, but I felt nothing I could say could help relieve the anguish he still suffered. I went to bed feeling a lot older than my years, and wondered how many of our generation, like the last, would carry the scars suffered from intense suffering for the rest of their lives.

When the Harvest Camp closed I was given two weeks holiday to recover. Pat was on leave and he suggested we should celebrate the end of the war in style. His parents had a London luxury flat in Herne Hill which Pat could use, and I was invited by Flo to have a holiday with her at her Highgate flat.

We decided to do some of the London Shows together as I had never seen much of London, but Flo and Pat knew their way around.

It was a magical holiday for me – quite apart from the wonderful stage sets of shows which quite dazzled me (by booking early we got 'stools' for the 'gods' most evenings), the lights of Piccadilly and the reflected lights in the Thames were a great excitement after the long years of no street lights. We met daily at Lyons Corner Houses, sometimes early enough for a good bacon breakfast; when we tired of walking there were art galleries where we could rest while enjoying the paintings. I quickly felt at home in London and greatly enjoyed a lunch at Pimm's when Pat introduced me to the city of bowler hats and rolled umbrellas.

Returning to work was an anti-climax, as I was at once informed that Michael Culham was to leave the War Ag. in October and Robert Hardy would take over as Chief Labour Officer. It surprised me how much this news upset me, but I suddenly realised that Michael had treated me as a respected colleague, rather than an employee. We shared similar views on most things, and ours was an easy relationship. Any worries I had I would share with Michael and he always cheered me on. I was fond of Robert Hardy, and we got on well, so I had no reason to mind the change, but I still realised that Michael had a charisma that was felt by all those who worked with him, and the job, already losing its former attraction for me, would never have the same appeal. I really must look around for a new job, either on the land or elsewhere.

Michael did not leave in October; he stayed until the end of November, and, in the way that I think God plans things, Joy Gane, Dairy Instructress of Sparsholt days, wrote to me with the offer of a job. Joy had just become Farm Manager of an Essex farm, owned by a gentleman farmer, Gerald Sketch. Joy said they needed help with a couple of cows and calves, and some general farm work. She asked whether I would like to apply for the job, as it would be fun for us to work together again. I did not hesitate, but applied right away, as the timing of the offer seemed to solve my problem of 'what next'. On 19th December 1945 I wrote my letter to Robert Hardy, telling him I would like my resignation to take effect from 11th January

1946. I received a kind letter of appreciation of my work in reply, and wishing me well in my future work. It was perhaps sensible, I felt, to give private farming another try to help me decide whether to stay with farming or return to hospital work, if that should be possible.

The Keevils invited me to their home to have a final family meal with them, and I was sad to leave them. Though I had added to Mr Keevil's problems, rather than being of much help to him latterly, he seemed quite genuinely sorry at the parting of our ways. Mrs Keevil had been a very good friend to me and I often had the joy of her company in the lorry when I was going to Swindon as she visited a sister there. Mr Keevil gave me a book token as a parting gift, and I never saw him again, though many years later Mrs Keevil and I did meet again, to our mutual delight.

I knew I was going to miss the War Ag. greatly, as they were such rewarding years, despite the wartime hardships. Those were eventful years, and I had gained a lot from the experience, for which I was very grateful.

18 Hill Farm, Wickham Bishops

January - June 1946

PATRICK UNDERSTOOD MY WORRIES ABOUT returning to work on a private farm after all the excitement of the War Ag. days, where I had enjoyed the Supervisor role, and he had a cheering surprise in store for me. I received a letter from his mother inviting me to join Pat and parents at the 'Old Vicarage Guest House' in St. Columb Minor, near Newquay, for my two weeks' leave between jobs – a most effective way of sweeping away any worries about whether I was mad to return to working on a small farm instead of seeking peace-time work.

Pat met me in London and we caught the night train to Cornwall. It was a very slow journey with not much sleep, as there was much noisy loading and unloading at various stations, especially at Templecombe where milk churns galore seemed to get boarded. I received a warm welcome from Mr and Mrs Davy, and was shown to a cosy room. Over breakfast I found my host and hostess easy to be with.

In those two weeks Pat was cheerful company, and I was pleasantly surprised at the good weather we enjoyed in January and, though bracing, the Newquay beach walks, with huge Atlantic rollers alongside the beach, were a thrilling experience. From then on, a walk with my dogs along any beach when the sea became gigantic, waves pounding the shore, never failed to revive the joy of those wonderful Newquay winter seas. The invigorating beach walks each morning always ended with a rendezvous with Pat's parents at a sea-front cafe that served the most delicious hot doughnuts with coffee. I sometimes walked home with Pat's mother while Pat spent time with his father. On that holiday I was taken to see much of Cornwall, a truly picturesque county, and I felt refreshed in spirit as I returned home to face the challenge of becoming a farm labourer once more.

Patrick again gave me a pleasant surprise by turning up at Waterloo to see me across to my Essex train. As the train pulled out he gave me a little package. To my amusement it was a banana, the first I had seen for years. I shared it with the girl in my compartment, and how we relished every bite.

Joy Gane was at the station to see me to my digs at Newlands Bungalow, with Stan and Judy Edwards, and their four-year-old son, Peter. The bungalow was about a mile from the farm buildings, where I would work with some of the stock. I was glad I had thought to bring a bike. There was a sizeable apple orchard surrounding this modern and comfortable bungalow, and this was Mr Edwards' work. At Newlands Bungalow, the Edwards family were very welcoming. While with them I soon learned what a lot of work went into producing good fruit. The planting, fertilising, spraying and training of the young trees, controlling pests that damaged fruit and the careful picking and packaging of fruit for market kept Stan and Judy Edwards busy all the year round. Stan was very encouraging in saying how happy I would be working for Mr Sketch, a very generous and appreciative boss.

I went with Joy up to the farm to meet my new employer and his wife. Joy then suggested I might start work at 9.15 am on my first day, as she would be busy gleaning advice from her predecessor, about to leave Hill Farm to get married and take charge of a rather larger farm. Although Mr Sketch had plans to enlarge his farm, he was only then farming about two hundred acres. The staff consisted of Joy as Manager; the foreman, Mr Payne, who was quite elderly; Mr Cousins, also getting on in years, who had charge of the two heavy horses, Captain and Tulip. Charlie, the one young man, was the general farmhand. I was to have the care of the cows, heifers, one bull, and some pigs. I was glad my main concern was to be with the animals, but with general work for the rest. After my late start the first day, my hours were to be from 6.30 am to 5 pm.

My first day at the farm, 22nd February, 1946, Joy was waiting

Above left: Mr. Gerald Sketch with Mr. Payne (left), Mr. Cousins (centre) and Charlie in doorway. Above right: Joy Gane, new farm manager.

to take me round, naming fields and stock. Meta, Strawberry, and Karen were in milk – all were Ayrshires, but Karen not pedigree. The eighteen bulling heifers were to be sold with calves at foot, not being kept to build up a herd. Frank, the pedigree bull, was as good natured as any bull can be relied upon to be. A pedigree boar (I called him Frazer), and five pedigree Essex gilts, with forty-five offspring, were to be my concern also. I was happy at the prospect of looking after this modest animal family, and would have plenty of time to prepare foods and get in some general work as well. Joy told me that Mr Sketch was aiming to get another two hundred acres of farmland, and the five and a half acres of apple orchard were part of the farm, though actually two miles away.

I was warned I needed warm clothing as the north-easterly winds on that hill were very penetrating. Joy said the vet had recently moved from Scotland, and complained that he had never got warm since he had come to Essex. We lunched at the farmhouse with the Sketch family, and these were breaks full of fun and laughter. Joy was very amusing and had so infectious a laugh that we were soon all laughing till the tears rolled. It was a big thrill to have landed so happy a job.

Hill Farm was well named, being at the top of a hill commanding glorious views. The River Blackwater, running through the farm, attracted lots of swans and colourful wild ducks. An ancient engine, drawing three carriages, ran regularly to Whitham from a station near Newlands Bungalow, which proved very handy for shopping expeditions. While deciding whether or not to continue with a farming career, this seemed an ideal job. After a few days I settled in to a regular routine of work at the farm. On arrival at 6.30 I first fed the heifers with mangolds and hay and then the pigs, who started clamouring for food as soon as they heard me around. I milked the two cows, which only yielded about two gallons of milk. The farm cats were then around for their daily ration of milk, while I was putting some aside for the farmworkers. The remainder was poured into shallow pans after straining, for Mrs Sketch's butter making. I then cycled back down the hill to breakfast with the Edwards family, taking them their can of milk. I was allowed an hour off for breakfast before going back to clean the cowshed, groom the cows and clean the pig pens. Next I led out Frank, the bull, for a drink and his feed. Frank would then be taken to the field and tethered to graze with the cows.

One learns never to rely on a bull's good nature, however docile he may be, but I was relieved that Frank was easy to handle, as he was quite a large bull. The cowsheds and pig pens had been allowed to harbour soiled litter and I set to work to get these properly cleaned out and well disinfected – the animals looked better for being housed in clean quarters. I found plenty to do between milkings with food to mix and bag, and weaning some of the piglets, and getting the sows into a paddock after the poor things had had their noses ringed to save them rooting up all the ground.

Joy was busy with the outgoing farm manager, Jim, all my first week, going through farm records and finances, etc., but we met over lunch with the Sketches. Joy kept us laughing during much of the meal, and Mr Sketch seemed to enjoy her great ideas for improving the farm. We had an hour and a half for lunch. I was usually finished with work to be back in my digs by 5 for tea. It was all very leisurely and relaxed working for Mr Sketch but I found it quite a lonely role, having so little to do after my previous jobs. I was glad when four-year-old Judith Sketch sometimes came out on her tricycle to chat to me. Judith had an older brother at school who was twelve, and made himself useful on the farm when on holiday. Judith took a great interest in all that went on in the farmyard and amused me by telling me one morning, "I saw Frank making love to Meta today". Farm life evidently provided a natural and easy sex education for little ones.

Once Joy was again working with me, the pace of life quickened considerably. The farm men did not take very kindly to the speed with which she wanted work done. Joy was well-built, young and very strong and did not adopt a relaxed attitude to work. She liked to do everything at speed and never seemed to tire. She had great ideas for modernising the farm and had a vision of turning this farm into a model unit. Her ideas seemed to please Mr Sketch, but the farm men were not impressed, nor did they like her plans. I found myself wondering if I could ever keep pace with her, as I had not her stamina and felt I could not live up to her expectations for long, though I enjoyed working with her.

We set to work riddling potatoes from a large potato clamp, and as each took a turn at the handle, Joy kept urging us to speed up turning the handle, though the well loaded riddle was heavy work. Despite very cold weather, we were soon all sweating and Payne protested to Joy, "You're never happy unless you've got us all sweating all the time". I was thankful I was able to break off to go and milk the cows.

On Saturdays and Sundays I had free time apart from the feeding of stock and milking. It was a treat for me when Patrick came for a weekend. He was to start work on a farm in Whitchurch, Hampshire, and was interested to see what work I was doing at Hill Farm. Once

Mr. Payne, Peter Sketch and Joy: Riddling, bagging and weighing potatoes from the clamp.

Pat started farmwork, though we kept up a correspondence about our farming activities, we did not meet again until he visited me when I had a weekend in Bournemouth. He then came to tell me he was shortly to be married, so our ways parted. I was surprised how much I missed him, but it had been a cheering episode of happy memories after the depressing wartime years, and I still had a very good friend in Michael Buckdale. Michael was teaching in a school in Kent, but we often met in London and enjoyed the sights together at every opportunity.

Michael Culham turned up unexpectedly at my digs one night, at his usual visiting hour of midnight. This was an embarrassment, because we had all been asleep when he roused the household by ringing the bell so late. To restore quiet I agreed to accompany him to the village, as he was dropping off a passenger there. I did not realise it was a village some miles away – not Wickham Bishops, so I was away for nearly an hour. This was very worrying to the Edwards who wondered if I had been abducted, and they roused the Sketches to get their advice but I was back before they contacted the police!

It was fortunate that, when apologising to Stan and Judy about the worrying event in the night, they accepted my explanation about the eccentric hours my former employer always kept, and they made light of the disturbance since I was safe and not abducted, and I was grateful for their understanding. It was not so easy to explain away my night ride with a young man to the Sketch household. Joy ragged me mercilessly about my 'romantic' night, and there was a definite cooling in my relationship with Mr and Mrs Sketch. I wrote at once to Michael telling him of the great embarrassment he had caused me by disturbing quiet village folk in the middle of the night and told him never to repeat so late a visit. Michael had in fact come to tell me he wanted to start a holiday camp business, and hoped with my experience of Harvest Camps I might like to help in this. He even said he thought we could happily marry and go into it together. At that moment I was more interested in getting back to bed, but tried to respond light-heartedly, but kindly, explaining I was only just settling in to this farm job and could not leave so quickly. I received no reply to my letter, and was very shocked when I heard later from Sue Nathan that she had read in a paper of the sudden death of Michael in London. She was quite devastated, as were most of Michael's former colleagues.

Michael's death caused great sorrow to his many war-time colleagues, as his charismatic leadership as Labour Officer for Wiltshire War Agricultural Committee had cheered and inspired all employees to give of their best in their work as Michael never spared himself. As a good friend, he had certainly cheered me through many a rough time with his encouragement and regular visits. I was very sad at the way our friendship had ended. His practice of overworking for very long hours during the war years evidently took its toll as the war effort did for so many.

Good relations with the Sketch family were evidently restored, I decided, when one day I was called into the farmhouse to see television broadcasts had been restarted, having been suspended during the war. On a small screen, in a large cabinet, we watched a black and white broadcast of a ballet danced by Margot Fonteyn. It seemed quite miraculous for us to be in Essex watching the performance then actually taking place in London. I was thrilled to have been invited in to see this new wonder.

I found I had time on Sundays to get to church services in the village in the morning, and was pleased to find Mr Sketch also there acting as sidesman. I was very often given a lift back to my digs. Sometimes Judy and young Peter found time to come along too. At weekends I could usually fit in some shopping in Chelmsford or Colchester or Witham. Stan would sometimes ask me to take their car and drive Judy to the shops, and we both enjoyed these outings, though I never felt very confident at the wheel of a car, after my training and years of lorry driving, and it was a new experience driving in towns. I enjoyed cycling round the Essex lanes and, when returning to the bungalow from the farm at dusk, it was amusing to have bats galore flying round my head and often I would see owls dozily sitting on gateposts, surveying the evening scene.

Happy and carefree as these days were, I was getting restless, as the work was so much less demanding than previous jobs. I had too much time on my own to wonder what I should be doing about returning to peace-time activity. At twenty-six-years-old I would find it none too easy to start another career if I left it much longer in deciding to leave the land. Machines were now taking over the work of horses and men, so the WLA would not be needed much longer. Combine harvesters now meant that two men could harvest and thresh a field of corn in a day, doing away with gangs to stook and load and make ricks of corn to await a later threshing, which had involved us in weeks of work in pleasant happy company. These monstrous grumbling machines, rumbling noisily round a beautiful field of ripe, standing corn would quickly replace the hard work, and do away with that sense of achievement and the camaraderie we all so enjoyed at harvest, thought of as the 'crowning' of the year's work, and do away with employment for many youngsters keen on the outdoor life. Though considered progress, financial gain for the few seemed to be the most likely result. How thankful I was to have experienced life on the land before these machines took over.

It was working with Joy one day that finally gave me the necessary prod to decide to leave farming. Joy called me to help her to load two-and-a-half-hundredweight sacks of wheat grain on to a trailer. We got three on to the trailer, with some effort, as I was at a disadvantage in not being as tall as Joy. Then I told her she must get one of the men to help her with the rest. I had always seen it take three men to lift these sacks, two to get the bottom of the sack up, and one to push from behind, so felt it was mad for us to try it alone. Joy was disappointed with my effort, but she was far stronger than me. I decided that six years of manual labour were enough if I was to remain fit. When I talked it over with Stan and Judy that evening, they seemed sad that I was to leave, as we had become good friends, but felt it was a right move.

Mr Sketch was gracious and kindly in expressing regret that I had decided to give up farmwork, but while thanking me generously for my help, he agreed that I was wise to give serious consideration to training for less arduous work, now the emergency was over. He was pleased I was to stay until June as I could help with the start of haymaking, and he was likely to find difficulty in getting a new worker at that time of the year.

Joy and I were quite sorry to be parting, but Joy did feel the War Ag. years had taken the edge off my enthusiasm and energy, and I agreed. While Joy, I think, thought that work had given me a taste for administration, I felt the very long and arduous camp work, motor cycling and gang control had left me very tired and in need of a restful break.

When I had arrived at Hill Farm the WLA was reluctant to let Mr Sketch employ a Land Girl on his small farm, and was now unlikely to replace me, so Joy might well be happier with a young man to take over the stock. I was sad to leave the animals, but rejoiced at having had as happy an end to my farm work with Joy and the Sketch family as Cara and I had at the start of our farming experience. At the outset Dad had suggested that six weeks of farm work might well prove enough for us, before transferring to other work. I was as pleased as he was that I had gained so much from my six years.

As soon as my father heard I had handed in my resignation to Mr Sketch, he sent me a newspaper cutting about Emergency Almoner Training Courses, offering a one-year training to qualify for membership of the Institute of Almoners. At the same time I was offered a post as a War Ag. Labour Officer in Buckinghamshire. Having decided to leave the land I asked Mrs Methuen and Lady Catherine McNeil if they would mind me giving their names as referees if I applied for this social work course, since I had only had experience of social work on their Land Army welfare committee meetings while in Wiltshire. Those references were evidently responsible for my being accepted on to the course. Furthermore, I was later informed by Mrs Methuen that the Land Army Benevolent Fund were awarding me £100 towards the cost of the training. I was quite overwhelmed, never having had so large a cheque before. It was a relief to have my future career mapped out, though I knew I was not going to find the change very easy to adapt to.

Hill Farm 'family' all made my last weeks very happy, and on the last day Mr Sketch sought me out to give me my final wage, with a generous bonus, and with good wishes for the future. I found it very hard to believe my farming days had ended, but the holiday prospect cheered me on.

By this personal message I wish to express to you

GWENDOLINE ANNE HALL

my appreciation of your loyal and devoted service
as a member of the Women's Land Army from
June 1940   to   29th June 1946
Your unsparing efforts at a time when the victory
of our cause depended on the utmost use of the
resources of our land have earned for you the
country's gratitude.

Elizabeth R

19 Post Script –
Back To 'Civvy Street'

THE WOMEN'S LAND ARMY HEADQUARTERS, in accepting my resignation, informed me that I might apply for a 'Thank You' certificate from Her Majesty the Queen, if I so wished. I was happy to receive this reminder of my six years of Land Army membership. I was asked to return some of the uniform, so I happily packed up gumboots, ankle boots, breeches, dungarees and overalls, being careful to retain my government gratuity of the greatcoat, shoes and two shirts. (I derived amusement from a cartoon comment on this gratuity that appeared in the Land Girl Magazine, showing a Land Girl in coat and shoes, with the quotation, 'Blow blow, thou winter wind, thou art not so unkind as man's ingratitude.' A rather apt comment?)

I am sure many of us rejoiced at the thought of swapping dung-splashed dungarees for nice summer dresses once more. I was glad to retain the WLA armband showing our years of service. Every six months we received a red, embroidered, half-diamond felt to sew on the green arm band. After four years I received a new red arm band with four diamonds embroidered on it. I had added another three half-diamonds, and wondered if I could now receive a fourth to complete the last diamond, having joined in June 1940, but that was our training and not farm employment, so my arm band lacked that last half-diamond, alas.

Of greater value than the half-diamond was, of course, the wonderful store of memories afforded by those years of rewarding toil. I felt a great debt of gratitude was owed to the many farmers and country dwellers who were so kind to us raw recruits until we became of real use to them. Our efforts were accepted with such good humour and patience that any hardships were well outweighed by enjoyment.

Resettling temporarily into home life again was not easy. My brother Bill, now having arrived home after the long years abroad, suffered the break-up of his marriage, instead of the joyful reunion he had so longed for. Cara, demobbed from the WAAF, accepted the offer of a place at Cardiff University to take up a child care training course.

I was delighted to have the offer of a temporary home with relatives in Wallington to enable me to commute daily by train to London to attend the Almoner training course.

Soon I found myself crammed into the corner of a very over-crowded train, staring at the impossible legal jargon of the proposed new Health Service Act, pining for the fields and fresh air. I wondered who could have guessed I was in fact listening inwardly to my wonderful Corsham gang singing, "Give me land lots of Land and a starry sky above, don't fence me in", to which I silently responded now, "Bless them all, the long and the short and the tall". Yes indeed, Bless them all, Bless them all.

About the author: After Social Work training, and starting an Almoner Department in St. Lukes Hospital in Bradford, the author was married in 1951 to The Revd. Raymond Fountain. There followed eight years at Hildenborough, Kent; eleven years at St. Paul's Church, Barrow in Furness; seven years at All Saints Church, Faringdon, Oxfordshire, and four years at Ennerdale, Cumbria, before retiring to live in Seaford, East Sussex, where Raymond died in 1986. Their two daughters also live in East Sussex.

If you have enjoyed reading Land Girl, *you may like to see some other books published by Ex Libris Press in our Country Bookshelf series. These are as follows:*

GROWING WITH THE GRAIN
A farming story by Richard Mack
An evocative and humorous read, set in the early 1960s.
£4.95

POACHERS & POISONED OWLS
Tales of a Country Policeman's Wife by Romy Wyeth   £4.50

LETTERS FROM THE ENGLISH COUNTRYSIDE *Essays on rural topics from a master of the genre* by Ralph Whitlock; £4.95

THE SECRET LANE *A country story* by Ralph Whitlock; £4.95

MARCH WINDS & APRIL SHOWERS: *Country weather lore* by Ralph Whitlock; £3.50

O WHO WILL MARRY ME?
A Book of Country Love by Ralph Whitlock; £3.50

THE ROMANY WAY
A book about gypsies and their way of life by Irene Soper; £4.95

MY NEW FOREST HOME
A house and garden in the New Forest by Irene Soper; £4.95

VILLAGE PRACTICE
A year in the life of a country doctor's wife by Anne Stratford; £4.95

WINIFRED: *Her Childhood and early Working Life* by Sylvia Marlow; £4.50

CHRISTIANA AWDRY'S HOUSEHOLD BOOK *Eighteenth century recipes and household tips* by Margaret Jensen; £4.95

GRAN'S OLD-FASHIONED REMEDIES, WRINKLES & RECIPES by Jean Penny; £3.50

GRAN'S OLD-FASHIONED GARDENING GEMS
by Jean Penny; £3.50

MAISIE & ME: *A country childhood in the 1920s* by Stella Ashton; £3.95

Ex Libris Press books may be obtained through your local bookshop or direct from the publisher, post-free, at

1 The Shambles,
Bradford on Avon,
Wiltshire, BA15 IJS

Tel/Fax 01225 863595

In addition to the above books, Ex Libris Press also publishes books on the West Country and the Channel Islands. Please ask for our free, illustrated list.